WAY *of*
Karma

In the same series:

Thorsons WAY *of* **Chakras**
Caroline Shola Arewa

Thorsons WAY *of* **Crystal Healing**
Ronald Bonewitz, PhD

Thorsons WAY *of* **Meditation**
Christina Feldman

Thorsons WAY *of* **NLP**
Joseph O'Connor and Ian McDermott

Thorsons WAY *of* **Natural Magic**
Nigel Pennick

Thorsons WAY *of* **Psychic Protection**
Judy Hall

Thorsons WAY *of* **Reiki**
Kajsa Krishni Börang

Thorsons WAY *of* **Reincarnation**
Judy Hall

Thorsons WAY *of* **Shamanism**
Leo Rutherford

Thorsons WAY *of* **Tarot**
Evelyne Herbin and Terry Donaldson

Thorsons WAY *of* **Tibetan Buddhism**
Lama Jampa Thaye

Thorsons WAY *of* **Wicca**
Vivianne Crowley

Thorsons WAY *of* **Zen**
Martine Batchelor

WAY *of*
Karma

Judy Hall

Thorsons

Thorsons
An Imprint of HarperCollins*Publishers*
77–85 Fulham Palace Road
Hammersmith, London W6 8JB

The Thorsons website address is: www.thorsons.com

and *Thorsons* are trademarks of
HarperCollins*Publishers* Limited

Published by Thorsons 2002

1 3 5 7 9 10 8 6 4 2

© Judy Hall 2002

Judy Hall asserts the moral right to be
identified as the author of this work

A catalogue record for this book
is available from the British Library

ISBN 0 00 711809 0

Printed and bound in Great Britain by
Martins the Printers Limited, Berwick upon Tweed

Contents

Acknowledgements

The author would like to acknowledge the assistance of Bryan Gundle with translation and with explanations of kabalistic belief and karma viewed from the Jewish perspective. I would also like to thank all those who have taught me so much about karma over the years, including the clients who have been generous enough to share their experiences in print.

Introduction

Millions of people the world over follow the way of karma. Many of these people, especially those who practise eastern religions such as Hinduism, believe their lives are governed by their karma. To them, karma is fate or duty: what must be. They see their present life as the culmination of their former actions; their circumstances as the inevitable result of a causal chain stretching back into the past and forward into the future. However, karma is more complex than this.

Believers in karma almost inevitably also embrace the concept of reincarnation and former lives. The Buddha said: 'I saw how beings vanish and come to be again. I saw high and low, brilliant and insignificant, and how each obtained according to his karma a favourable or painful rebirth', but as Sogyal Rinpoche, a Tibetan lama, has pointed out: 'karma is both the power latent within actions, and the results our actions bring.'[1] Stressing that karma is not predestination but rather it is a chain of cause and effect, he quotes the Buddha: 'Karma creates all, like an artist, karma composes, like a dancer.'

It is not necessary to believe in reincarnation to accept karma. Karma can arise and have its consequences in the present life. Anyone who follows the precepts: 'Do as you would be done by' or 'Do unto others what you would have them do unto you' is actually following the way of karma, whether they know it or not.

WAY of

> ### Karma
> *The process by which we meet what we have created previously.*

> ### Soul
> *The eternal principle which passes from life to life and which is a vehicle for karma.*

> ### Reincarnation
> *Successive lives lived in different bodies. Reincarnation postulates that the soul of someone now living previously inhabited a different physical body. At the death of the earlier body the soul continued in another dimension and was (at some stage) incarnated in a new physical body.*

For those who believe in karma as fate, karma is unalterable, fixed and unchanging. Some Hindus, for example, regard karma as 'duty'. It is what they must do, the path that is mapped out for them. To other people, however, karma is flexible, encompassing room for growth. For these people, karma is a guide to their spiritual intention. It is the memory of the soul in action (more usually known by the Sanskrit word *dharma* or way). To such people, karma is not only a law of retribution but also of compensation and recompense, and growth. A continuity principle, it creates equilibrium in their lives. A balancing process that involves action and reaction, response and reparation, it is nevertheless dynamic and creative. For all such believers, karma explains their life circumstances and any suffering they may be undergoing.

Karma is an ancient concept. It is set out in the Hindu scriptures and in Buddhist writings but the concept appears, in different guises, within other world religions. *Karma* is a Sanskrit word meaning work or action. It is an on-going process. Something is set in motion and has repercussions. This can occur on many levels and in ways that are subtle or gross, immediate or long term. Karma arises not only out of action but out of thoughts, attitudes and desires. It is the sum total of all that the soul has experienced in its cycle of incarnations – although in Buddhism, for instance, there is no notion of a separate *soul* moving from life to life but rather karmic seeds and potentials passing from moment to moment. The concept of karma is usually associated with rebirth, but this is not necessarily so. The past is the past, whether it belongs to another life or to the present one. Actions have consequences and time has little relevance in the working out of karma.

> **Other Lives**
> *The previous lives that a soul has lived upon the earth and in other planes of existence.*

Karma implies *continuous* causality, what is experienced now being the result of personal or collective prior action. Karma does not decay or become inoperative, but it may go into suspension until the conditions are right for it to 'ripen'. The connection between an action and a reaction may be immediately apparent but this is not always so. Karma can be a delayed reaction. A soul may have karma to deal with from a lifetime seemingly many hundreds of years from the present incarnation. Conditions may not have been right for the soul to deal with the karma before. It may have had to develop certain strengths and insights first. Cultural, economic or environmental factors may not have been right. The people it needed to incarnate with to deal with the karma may not have been ready. Notwithstanding, time is not linear and chronological, it only seems that way from the perspective of earth. So the karma may have *appeared* to take a long time to come around but in the context of eternal time, it has passed in the blink of an eye. On the other hand, karma appears to be speeding up. Many people now find that the consequences of yesterday's actions are returning almost immediately, and they do not need to wait for another life.

Even the smallest of actions or the briefest of thoughts can produce karma. Every moment is pregnant with its consequences. These consequences may not necessarily be 'bad'. Good karma matures in the same way that more negative forms do. The Buddha said: 'Do not overlook tiny good actions, thinking they are of no benefit; even tiny drops of water in the end will fill a huge vessel.'[2]

People tend to view karma as punitive but it is actually neutral and non-judgemental. What may be termed 'karmic misfortune' is simply the result of past actions coming round again to be balanced out. It is a tool for teaching the consequences of actions – past and present. It is through karma that the soul learns and progresses.

Regression
Directly re-experiencing the past through hypnotic means or some other form of altered awareness.

> **Life Reading**
> *An impression of past lives and karmic causes*
> *received by a psychic when tuning into the person*
> *concerned.*

In the present day, many people explore their karma through regression to past lives. In re-experiencing their former lives, they understand the forces operating in the present. They can see the actions, thoughts or intentions that set a chain of events in motion. The regression experiences of people all over the world, which are supported by the 'life readings' carried out by the American seer Edgar Cayce and other psychics such as myself, show that karmic manifestation may either occur as a pattern of ingrained actions, attitudes and beliefs which repeat through a cycle of lives; or can involve 'swinging between two opposite extremes' until a balance is reached.

In the first case, for instance, a woman may have had an abusive experience in one life which caused her to fear men. In her next few lives the fear may become ever more deeply ingrained and, because what is feared most is attracted by the soul, she may have experiences that reiterate and reinforce her original fear. This fear could result in taking up a position of extreme militant, lesbian feminism in the present life – wanting to do away with men altogether perhaps – or in her becoming the eternal spinster. In former times, she could well have become a nun.

On the other hand, the karma could manifest physically as an inability to engage in sexual activity, inorgasmia or vaginal spasm being typical conditions associated with such a fear. These conditions are more properly defined as dis-ease rather than disease. She may even swing between male and female incarnations in an effort to avoid her fear, living lives as a man where the fear is a karma-in-suspension. Eventually, however, her soul will engineer an opportunity for her to face up to the anxiety. This may be through an extreme manifestation of the circumstances she fears but there are less destructive ways of dealing with this karma. She may fall in love with a gentle man who is able to show her another way of being; or may find herself meeting a man who portrays qualities different from those she has experienced in other lives. Eventually, her fear will be healed.

In the 'swinging between two extremes' manifestation, the soul experiences one end of the spectrum in one life and then rebounds to the other extreme in the next life. So, for example, a man who is overly sensual, lustful and aggressive in chasing women in one life, may then swing to the opposite extreme of celibacy or timidity in relationships in another life. Such swings will continue until a balance is found.

'Unfinished business' draws people back into incarnation time and time again but karma can change and, as regression experience shows, there can be karmic 'accidents' – although what appears to be an accident may not actually be so. In the first instance, a very strong desire on the part of another person, for example, could pull a soul into a birth that was not pre-ordained. That soul would be being 'sucked into incarnation' before it was ready. From regression experiences, such 'accidents' are rare but nevertheless they do occur.

Edgar Cayce gave many examples in his life readings of seeming accidents that actually brought karma, and soul intention, to the sur-face. In one, a boy was paralyzed in an automobile accident at the age of 16. When Edgar Cayce later read his past lives, he picked out two as particularly relevant. In one, the boy had been a military officer of great courage and determination during the American Revolution. The qualities he had developed then were of great assistance to him in overcoming the consequences of his 'accident'. However, Cayce also identified an earlier life as the root cause of the 'accident'. Here the young man had been a self-indulgent Roman soldier who 'glorified' in the suffering inflicted on the early Christians – which he actively took part in as he was one of those who fought the Christians in the arena. According to Cayce, the man had seen much suffering but made light of it and the deep religious conviction that lay behind it. Now it was time for him to suffer not as retribution but so that he could understand how it felt and also how the 'purposefulness' of those he had mocked had given them the strength to endure. Dr Gina Cerminara, who reported this case history, closely studied the Cayce files and concluded that 'some inner imperceptible line of force is operative even in the sudden chaos of accident such that karmic dues are accurately apportioned.'[3]

Karma has been said by some to be a 'get-out clause' by which a person can do whatever he or she wills in the present life, with the view that he or she can always pay for it in a later life. Few believers in karma would wish to take this path as they would recognize that consequences would inevitably follow. Such a view does not take account of the purpose of karma – which is to ultimately move off the karmic wheel. Nor can karma be used as an excuse. 'I can't help it, it's my karma', keeps the incarnating soul stuck and impedes spiritual growth. And, as the Buddha pointed out, not everything is attributable to karma. The student who fails exams through laxity cannot blame past karma for the failure. The person who makes an ethical or moral choice which is not in accord with the common good may possibly be acting out of past conditioning, which could be called karma, but is equally likely to be acting out of motives of self-interest, which will *accrue* karma but will not be caused by it. There is an element of personal responsibility within karmic manifestation which demands that the incarnating soul should own what he or she does and experiences, rather than simply blaming karma from the past for everything.

What one experiences in the future *will be* the result of present action. What is put in motion now has repercussions later. In the modern understanding of karma, the exercise of choice and free will is possible. Therefore, the doctrine of karma adds a dimension of personal responsibility to 'destiny' and anyone who takes reincarnation seriously is likely to 'want to get things right this time', rather than to accept fatedness or to act in a way for which reparation has to be made at some future date. In other words, they follow the soul's urge towards perfection and reintegration into the divine whole.

A Karmic Definition

Karma is cause and effect operating in everyday life. What is set in motion has consequences. Karma is purposeful, concerned with growth and evolution, rather than punishment. A balancing force, it is neutral and all-embracing and has many manifestations. Karma operates at different levels, from the personal to the universal. It shows where balance is needed and may involve reparation, or retribution for past actions, and reward and restitution. Karma does not simply stem from actions and events. It encompasses intention, words, attitudes, thoughts and desires – and ingrained habits.

Note: The majority of the karmic teachings and insights in this book arise from the Western Mystery Tradition and regression or Far Memory work. They draw on, but do not strictly adhere to, Buddhist teachings. They are eclectic not sectarian.

ONE

TYPES OF
Karma

There are many types of karma, and these operate at the personal, group, collective and cosmic level. Not all types of karma will be active at any one time. The soul usually works on two or three karmic themes during a lifetime but may concentrate on only one if it involves a major life lesson such as a chronic illness or self-sacrifice.

Three things strongly affect karma: desire, purpose and grace:

Desire (often called craving or wilfulness) is a powerful creator of karma. The human mind has a tendency towards intense attachment arising out of desire. According to Buddhist philosophy, attachment is what underlies rebirth. Desire is a compulsion, involuntarily followed. What is wanted, needed or craved brings about a situation that will provide it – not always a beneficial experience. The soul may be learning to let go of that desire and the pattern it continually creates. The other major attachments are to emotions and mental constructs – which are still a form of desire. The strength of desire can transcend death and pull a soul back into incarnation to deal with unfinished business or to recreate once again a situation where the desired object can, so it seems, be achieved. Desire keeps the karmic wheel turning.

Purpose is soul intention. It is what the soul incarnates to do and can operate at different levels. Purpose has to do with the soul's evolution, the incorporation of qualities and experiences it has identified as being required for further soul growth. It is often vocational or spiritual. Purpose can overcome destructive desires, as when an addict goes into recovery, and it can also compensate for difficult karma.

Grace strengthens purpose and helps it to manifest. Grace is an offer from the highest part of being to release karma. Opinions differ as to whether that 'highest part' is of oneself or something other. Edgar Cayce, for instance, believed it came from God and not from oneself, whilst I believe that it comes from one's own higher Self and agree with Hindus that the highest part of the soul *is* divine.

Grace operates when enough has been done or when forgiveness is practised. There are some lessons or situations that simply cannot be continued with, perhaps because another person is concerned who is unwilling to learn. The concept of grace says that, when the soul has done all it can, it can let it go and no further karma will accrue. Grace also comes into play when a soul learns to forgive and let go the past – or seeks forgiveness for itself.

Karmic Levels

Personal Karma is carried from life to life by an individual soul. It has been created in the past and the soul incarnates to deal with it in the present or to fulfil its purpose. There are many examples throughout this book of the manifestation of personal karma.

Group or Racial Karma belongs to a group of people. The group can vary in size from a family, or group of friends, to a tribe, a race or a country. Most people who become involved in group karma will have incarnated into that group before but this is not always so. People incarnate into a group because they have personal karma with the family, or the race, etc, and have to work that karma out, or because they have the intention of helping to alleviate karma from within the group even though they had no part in setting it up. However, souls may 'accidentally' get caught up in group karma with which they have no connection. The situation may or may not resonate with their own personal karma. Group karma overcomes the individual.

So, a soul who has no aggressive karma may nevertheless become caught up in a war or other mass movement, for instance, simply because it has incarnated into that group at that time.

Annie Besant, one of the founders of Theosophy, expressed the opinion in her *Study in Karma* that a colonizing nation such as England was guilty of much cruelty in the way it took over lands belonging to others. She stated that thousands of people would have perished prematurely during the conquest and subsequent colonization of such lands. According to her, all these souls would have a karmic claim against England. However, England, as the colonizing country, would carry a racial karma and would owe a karmic debt to the colonized countries; the inhabitants of England at that time would have a group karmic responsibility and some would have personal karma within the overall group. This claim would operate on a racial or collective level, and a personal claim against those who perpetrated the atrocities would also be present.

In her view, this resulted in thousands of people being drawn to the English slums 'providing a population of congenital criminals, of non-moral and feeble-minded people'.[1] It is not clear what the basis for her statement is but, as she refers to the people whose land was taken as 'savage tribes', she is perhaps expressing the view of her time (early-twentieth century) that everyone who was not a Christian was a 'savage heathen' although she, through her Theosophy, admired the philosophy of the Indian people who had, of course, also come under the domination of England. Notwithstanding, her answer to the collective or racial responsibility imposed on England by its colonial acts was that the country should educate and train the people who had reincarnated into the slums, 'thus quickening their evolution and lifting them out of their natural savagery.'[2]

Racial karma may also lie in specific qualities attaching to a race. Dr Hiroshi Motoyama, a scientist and Shinto priest, who works extensively with karma, says that Japan, for instance, has a karma of obstinate loyalty and patriotism. He points out that the defeat of Japan during the Second World War was the first time this nation experienced defeat in its long history. In a somewhat prophetic statement (his book was published in 1992) he says that he is concerned about the karmic seeds that Japan was then sowing during an era of prosperity. He would no doubt see the economic collapse at the end of the twentieth century as reaping those karmic seeds.[3]

Dr Motoyama recounts how he went to a small town in California. He was aware of considerable confusion and unrest amongst the inhabitants – mainly of English or Russian descent. The town was situated in the immensely old Redwood country and the major source of work was felling these ancient trees. The original inhabitants, Native American Indians, had revered these trees, but they had been brutally murdered by the first white settlers and carried what he describes as 'ferocious animosity' towards white people, particularly the Russians who had first settled there.

Dr Motoyama realized that these original inhabitants were now being reincarnated as the present inhabitants, causing enormous confusion. They were white on the outside, and Indian on the inside. It was his conclusion that they were collectively carrying the guilt of having murdered their former selves. If Dr Motoyama is correct in his reading of the situation, then there is another element to this. They are now engaged in destroying the environment that they had so respected in the past. This must create an enormous conflict in their spiritual selves which will no doubt have karmic repercussions.

5

Collective Karma is the karma of the human race. It arises from all that has gone before. Although positive collective karma is generated, negative collective karma is what creates problems for future generations. This arises out of wars, territorial disputes, genocide, religious intolerance and enforced conversion, exile and persecution. No one is responsible for collective karma in the sense of having personally created it, although souls may have been part of its source in conflict, purges, ideologies and other mass movements. Certain people incarnate with the intention of taking on part of this collective karma and clearing it for the wider whole.

Collective karma does not only relate to the acts of humankind. Nature too has its place in manifesting collective karma. The theosophist Annie Besant asserted that seismic changes such as earthquakes, volcanoes, floods, and national catastrophes like plagues and famine were actually cases of collective karma. It was her contention that they were created by 'great streams of thoughts and actions' arising out of the influence of a nation's past. Anthroposophist Rudolf Steiner, on the other hand, saw such events as arising out of a much more cosmic struggle between darkness and light.

Nowadays, with television reaching into the most inaccessible places, collective karma is touching everyone. It can no longer remain a remote event for which no one takes responsibility. So, when news broadcasts show a war in Bosnia or Kosovo, for instance, together with its effect on children and adults, 'ordinary people' band together to send aid – and to work for peace. This could be seen as part of an awakening consciousness of shared humanity, what some spiritual movements would call recognizing the divine spark within each person. It is a step in the evolution of humankind, the flowering of cosmic karma.

Cosmic Karma is the need for the whole cosmos to grow and to evolve. It is the spiritual purpose which can override all other karmas. If Christians believed in karma, they would say that Jesus' incarnation was an example of cosmic karma in action. They believe that he incarnated to take away the sins of the world, an act of redemptive karma on behalf of the whole.

Types of Karma

Attitudinal or Affective: Past intransigent attitude, ingrained behaviour, intractable or habitual emotional stance, results in spiritual and physical 'dis-ease'.

Communication: How and what has been communicated has repercussions.

Hypocrisy: Having said one thing, or done things a certain way, and yet believed something different, or taken an 'anything for a quiet life' approach. Arises out of lack of spiritual conviction and inner truth, or betrayal of truth.

Ideological: Attachment to a belief has consequences, especially if imposed on other people. The belief may be religious, philosophical or secular.

In-suspension: Not manifesting in the present.

In-the-making: Each thought, deed, action and belief in the present creates future karma.

Merit: Reward for talents developed, lessons learned, insights put into practice.

Mockery: Debasing other people's afflictions, thoughts, beliefs or actions and not valuing another's pathway.

Organic: Reflects injuries or conditions from other lives.

Pacts and Promises: Vows and assurances given in the past.

Recompense: Reward or recognition for actions in the past, or for sacrifices made.

Redemptive: Intention of helping others or doing something for the world including clearing collective karma.

Relationship: Arises in families, love affairs, friendships and business relationships.

Retributive: 'Boomerang' effect of former actions or debts to be paid. 'The punishment fits the crime.'

'Sins of Omission and Commission': Consistent refusal to take action, or to learn a lesson; or persistent inappropriate action.

Symbolic: Present-life condition symbolizes what was done in the past.

Technological: The use, or misuse, of technology in the past.

Treadmill: Destructive patterns that have not been outgrown.

Work and Vocational: carried over from activities in former lives. Can be positive or negative.

The different categories of karma may apply at a personal, group, racial or collective level. They will be explored in greater depth through the remainder of this book, with particular reference to how they manifest through the incarnations of an individual soul.

Karmic Sources

The case histories used in this book draw on hundreds of psychic and astrological karmic readings carried out by myself in over 25 years of karmic exploration and on the regression experiences or past life memories of my clients. (Identities and locations have been disguised to protect client's confidentiality.) I have also used case histories from the published work of Edgar Cayce, arguably one of the largest and most complete studies of karma available today (see Appendix); and consulted the work of Rudolf Steiner and many others. The case histories have been selected because they exemplify universal experiences. Many people will share almost exactly the same past-life experience and karmic cause – although individual details differ, the overall particulars will be the same. Time and again I have read through five or six books on past-life or between-life regression and have been able to identify, across a wide geographical spectrum, experiences that I have shared with my own clients. To me, although it does raise some questions that I have explored elsewhere about the validity of every past-life memory (see *Deja Who*), it also points overwhelmingly to the universality of the themes and causes that run through karmic experience.

TWO

KARMIC
Themes

There are certain karmic themes that weave throughout human interaction over aeons of time. Suffering is a universal karmic theme but there are others such as justice, power, betrayal, forgiveness and love that are equally ubiquitous. Themes work throughout individual lives, and intertwine through the history of a race or a land.

A soul may not necessarily be involved with a particular theme in each and every life but, when reviewed, a *leitmotiv* runs through the soul's entire experience like a river which sometimes goes underground only to surface again when the terrain is right. It is as though the soul has become immersed in that theme, and must view and experience it from all sides before resolving it. Sometimes the soul seems stuck – either in the negative or positive aspect. At other times, it swings between two extremes within it: persecutor and persecuted, for instance. An intense encounter with the theme may be followed by a few lives' rest, but the soul will then pick up the theme again and again until it is completed. Most souls will be working with several themes, some or all of which will be apparent in any one life.

Many karmic themes run counter to each other and frequently work down through lives as pairs of opposites. 'Power-over' and control issues are the antithesis of empowerment and autonomy; betrayal is accompanied by the opportunity for forgiveness as the betrayer becomes the betrayed. Poverty consciousness, which is based on a deep lack of self-worth, has to be turned to abundance so some lives will be of deprivation, others of wealth. The wealth is not recompense for the poverty. It is a challenge to see how the soul handles both extremes.

Other themes complement each other. Someone working on love tends to incorporate intimacy, companionship, unconditional love and acceptance into several lives, but may well also find that cruelty, betrayal and loss are inextricably bound up within the love theme.

Major Karmic Themes:

- *Suffering and dis-ease*
- *Forgiveness*
- *Persecution and betrayal*
- *Exile and belonging*
- *Abandonment and loss*
- *Scapegoating*
- *Victim–martyr–saviour–persecutor*
- *Guilt*
- *Love*
- *Justice*
- *Loss of or attaining individuality*
- *Control versus freedom*
- *Deprivation and abundance*
- *Fear that 'there will never be enough'*
- *Security*
- *'Niceness' versus authenticity and congruence*
- *Attachment and detachment*
- *Independence and dependence*
- *Intimacy*
- *Self-worth*
- *Power-over and empowerment*
- *Finding wholeness*
- *Nurturing*
- *Acceptance*
- *Restriction and release*
- *Debts and promises*
- *Spirituality*

Suffering and Disease

In the Eastern view, all suffering is based on karma – in other words it is a punishment for the past. In the Western view, however, suffering and disease may be a way of developing new soul qualities or of making reparation for what has gone before. Dis-ease too may be a learning experience rather than karmic retribution. Notwithstanding, souls may reincarnate with spiritual dis-ease that manifests physically, or with repeating patterns of illness, ingrained attitudes or other karmic experiences that lead to suffering and dis-ease (see Chapters Five and Six). Souls may also experience these themes through those close to them such as family and friends, or through working with others to alleviate these conditions.

Forgiveness

Forgiveness is a powerful karmic lesson but one that is not easily learned and so may take many lifetimes to work out. Superficial forgiveness is easy, but ineffective. Forgiveness emerges out of a struggle to accept things as they are, to see the imperfections and embrace them. It is an opportunity to practise unconditional love and compassion. Forgiveness transforms deep, toxic feelings of rage and pain, and their karmic repercussions. The soul may need to forgive itself or others. It may need an opportunity to bring a festering secret into the light and look on its bearer with compassion. It may need to learn how to let go of apportioning blame, or of a deeply-ingrained sense of abandonment. If this is the case, opportunities will arise in various guises.

There are four stages to forgiveness and the soul may work on all of them within one lifetime or during a progression of lives. Letting go is the first, refusing to dwell on the wound or to apportion blame or plan revenge. Refraining from punishment is the second stage. This lessens the opportunity for resentment to fester and reduces guilt. It allows generosity of spirit to flourish. The soul must then move on to forgetting. Not in a superficial way but in a way that lays the matter to rest, puts it out of the mind and ensures that it is not carried over to another incarnation. Forgiveness then follows, for both parties. This gives up the feeling of being owed anything – a powerful manifestor of karmic reaction – and lets go of the sense that anyone else is responsible for personal pain. At this stage the other person can be thanked for their part in the karmic lesson and the soul has nothing holding it to the past. It is free to move on. At its highest level, forgiveness recognizes there is nothing to forgive. It was all grist to the evolutionary mill.[1]

Persecution and Betrayal

Themes naturally fall into groups. Forgiveness, persecution and betrayal go alongside scapegoating, exile and banishment, as do abandonment and loss. Many people do not get the opportunity to escape the results of betrayal or persecution. A soul planning to leave a country to avoid persecution runs the risk of betrayal. Many people unconsciously expect betrayal because of their previous karmic experiences, and may well attract it again and again as part of a karmic lesson. When a new country is reached, there is a feeling of exile, of 'not belonging'. The soul may have a deep-seated expectation of rejection and does not fit into the society. So long as the soul is unable to forgive those responsible for the 'banishment', the theme will recur, with variations, over and over again. Similarly, a soul may well find itself being scapegoated time and time again. He or she becomes the focus of anger, or is blamed for the ills of the group – or of a person. Blame and judgement play an enormous part in complex karmic interactions which hold souls in relationship until one soul stops holding the other responsible for how he or she is feeling, or for the things that have gone wrong, or for however else the theme has been playing out.

The need for forgiveness often arises out of betrayal. Being betrayed is perhaps the most painful of all wounds, and the guilt of having been the betrayer haunts the soul through many lifetimes. If forgiveness is not possible, then the resultant bitterness and guilt erode the soul. It as though the sense of self is poisoned. The antidote to betrayal, whatever role the soul took, is forgiveness.

Victim–Martyr–Saviour

One of the most pervasive themes is the victim–martyr–saviour syndrome. It frequently begins by someone trying to save the world – or an individual person – but the scenario quickly turns the 'saviour' into the victim or the martyr. Equally, a victim can metamorphose into a persecutor who makes life miserable for a former tormentor. Whilst there are subtle variations of this theme played out in families, marriages, jobs and vocations, the underlying question remains the same: 'What did I do to deserve this?' Once the soul realizes that it is creating the situation, then changes can be made, but until that realization is reached, many lives will be played out in the victim role.

However, there are more serious karmic causes behind the eternal victim. Humankind has, unfortunately, a history of persecuting or scapegoating anyone with different views. There are some souls who take on this role intentionally, trying to change how humanity thinks, or practising redemptive karma. There are others who get caught up in a pattern of victimhood or martyrdom from which they find it impossible to escape. And there are those who persecute.

Breaking free from this cycle involves learning lessons of tolerance, acceptance, open-mindedness and valuing each person as they are.

Guilt

Guilt is an insistent and insidious karmic theme. The soul feels culpable, responsible. Some souls seem to suffer from 'existential guilt'. Its source is buried so deep that the guilt seems all pervasive, always there. Deep inside, the soul craves punishment for whatever this 'badness' was. When dreadful things happen, this is the soul who assumes it has deserved them because of the past. There are people who are always apologizing, they feel guilt over the slightest thing. Such people suffer from other people's guilt, taking it on themselves. They feel they are responsible for everyone else as well as themselves. Other souls have one or two – or more – acts for which they find it hard to forgive themselves. For many souls in past lives the theme was *'Mea culpa'*: 'I am guilty, I am responsible.' Such culpability often arises out of religious lives or religious conditioning. The guilt is inappropriate but the soul has not let go.

There are people, however, who, in the past, have committed atrocities and offences. They may, or may not, have been punished for these. But they go on punishing themselves. They too need to let go and practise forgiveness. Looking on oneself and others with compassion brings about forgiveness and heals the soul.

Love

Understanding and practising universal love is a major soul lesson. In the process a soul may well have to experience the difference between loneliness and aloneness, balancing companionship with intimacy and emotional detachment. There may well be lifetimes where dislike and hatred are faced and others where cruelty and kindness come to the fore. The soul who is on the pathway of universal love will have lifetimes to practise both letting go and compassion, and will then work on merging back into the divine.

Justice

The soul cannot know justice without having experienced injustice and so will have experienced lifetimes when it learns about injustice in all its aspects before returning to work on bringing justice to all. One of the most important aspects of justice is that of karmic 'rightness'. Learning not to blame, not to punish and not to criticize but instead allowing the soul to learn in its own way is fundamental to this pathway. As is a close exploration of exactly what 'fairness' entails. Does it mean allowing every soul exactly the same opportunity – treating them as all the same – or does it mean treating each soul according to its own unique self? This theme will take the soul into some difficult byways as it explores the answers.

Loss of, or Attaining, Individuality

Recognizing one's own unique self is part of the theme of individuality, as is realizing that one is a part of the whole and finding a way to return to that wholeness. Issues around self-worth and self-confidence often arise as this theme works its way through lives, which may also include experience of being owned body and soul by someone else – the master/slave experience – and its opposite.

Control Versus Freedom

Control and empowerment are huge karmic contrasts. Whilst exploring these themes the soul looks at conforming to the rules or the norm and at challenging these. It explores issues around assertion and use of the will, and of aggression and restriction. It will have experiences of independence, dependence and interdependence. It will find itself in power-over situations and has to seek empowerment and release from all that has held it back in the past.

Deprivation and Abundance

The fear that there will never be enough and the need to find inner security are closely linked to deprivation and abundance, but may also be part of love issues (see Chapter Nine). Fundamental lessons around deprivation often arise from 'poverty consciousness' which in turn comes out of believing that there will never be enough. It can have its roots in neglect or in extreme poverty or lack of love, or in lives intended to help the soul look at security issues. There will no doubt have been lives of over-abundance and those of extreme deprivation at all levels. One of the most vital lessons for the soul is to find inner security, based on the recognition of itself as an eternal being, rather than the spurious security of material possessions. The soul must also develop a notion of abundance which is not based purely on financial wealth but which embraces joy and spiritual generosity. The soul who is on this pathway may also explore nurturing and parenting issues.

'Niceness' versus authenticity

Pervasive karma can arise out of the 'people pleaser' archetype. A people pleaser is someone who tries to please all the people all the time – and usually ends up pleasing no one. This person believes that 'niceness' is preferable to being authentic, and has to develop congruence between inner and outer qualities. A congruence that can only come from fully knowing and accepting oneself and not being afraid to show this to the world. Along the way the need to recognize the difference between spurious 'humbleness' and true humility can arise.

Attachment and Detachment

Karmic bonds can carry forward over many lives and often include issues of dependence versus independence. Some attachment is constructive and positive – where one soul undertakes to aid the development of another, for instance, and where parents commit to nurturing their children, or where a couple comes together for a specific purpose. These bonds may be 'time specific', as with children who reach adulthood and then need to be related to in a different way to when they were young. However, some attachments are simply habits that have been carried forward and it may well be time for the souls to separate (see Chapter Nine). Detachment may also be a necessary lesson where one person has felt responsible for the well-being of another, or where a soul feels that someone else 'owes them something'. If a soul has been too dependent on another person, or has always been fiercely independent, then the challenge is to experience the opposite polarity. The lesson may then be to move into interdependence where two souls have an equal, supportive relationship rather than a dependent one.

Lessons around attachment and detachment also occur with ideas, beliefs, substances and places, attachment or desire being one of the main causes of karma.

Intimacy

Couples often incarnate together again and again as they work upon intimacy issues, but the theme is also pertinent to single souls who find it difficult to open themselves to close relationship with another soul. Commitment issues often go alongside those of intimacy.

Self-worth

Lack of self-worth can be a deeply ingrained karmic burden that a soul carries from life to life. The challenge is to develop a sense of inner worth and value that allows the soul fully to develop its potential.

Power-over and Empowerment

Power is a karmic theme which can have extensive ramifications. The soul may well have experienced abuse and misuse of power – either as victim or perpetrator – throughout many lifetimes. Indeed, the soul may have come to feel inwardly powerless and helpless and, therefore, attracts exactly those scenarios in the present life. On the other hand, the soul may be 'power hungry' and determined to hold all the power in relationships, business, etc, in which case it will attract 'power-over' scenarios. The soul's challenge is to become empowered, recognizing that power is not 'mine' but rather something that flows through the soul and is used appropriately.

Finding Wholeness

Integrating all the parts of the soul and its past experiences, and fully developing potential, brings wholeness, as does recognizing that the soul has a divine origin. Souls may go through many spiritual or religious experiences on the road to wholeness.

Nurturing

In both men and women, the need to nurture may be a powerful urge that demands satisfaction. It is usually expressed in other lives through caring for children or those who need help. On the other hand, if the soul has been driven by this urge through many lifetimes, it may now be time for the soul to recognize that there are other ways to nurture – just as realizing that creativity can be a non-biological process may be important. For many souls, especially those who have been taught always to put other people first, it may be a revelation to learn that self-nurturing is both necessary and advisable.

Acceptance

The acceptance here is of both oneself and others. The need for acceptance drives many souls into actions which are not totally congruent with their spiritual purpose or inner feelings. It can also lead to repressing large parts of oneself in an effort to be acceptable either to parents, authority figures or peers. Souls who have experienced bigotry, or who have practised this in the past, may carry particularly strong lessons around acceptance in the present life.

Restriction and release

Many souls have experienced conditions of severe restriction in the past. This may have come about through personal circumstances such as poverty or lack of education, authoritarian parenting, or repressive regimes and the like. The soul may also have been held back by lack of belief in itself and its abilities. The challenge in the present life is to release anything which has held the soul back from fulfilling its potential.

Debts and promises

Karmic promises, burdens and duties often lock a soul into a relationship with another. Karmic enmeshment can arise when one soul feels that it owes another something, or where a soul feels that it is owed reparation or repayment for 'services rendered'. This theme can arise between parents and child, lovers, business partners, and in many other interactions. There may be a karmic need to rescind a vow, to release from a promise, or to recognize that enough is more than sufficient when it comes to repaying a debt.

Spirituality

Many souls come into incarnation with a strong spiritual purpose. In other experiences this may well have entailed lives as monks or nuns but in the present life the challenge may be to live in the world in a spiritual way rather than withdrawing entirely. One of the major karmic tasks facing a soul is the recognition of its divine roots and its reintegration with that source of its being.

THREE

KARMIC
Causes

In the traditional, fatalistic approach to karma, the rule is 'an eye for an eye, a tooth for a tooth'. Actions rebound on the perpetrator. If a man murders, he will become a victim; if he injures, he will be injured; if he holds untenable attitudes, he will himself become an example of what he despises. In other words, what a man is arises out of his past actions and determines his destiny. In this view of karma, what is set in motion is fixed and unmoving. This notion of fate is strongly interwoven with the Hindu view of karma. In Tibetan Buddhism, negative karma can be purified and the future changed. As Sogyal Rinpoche puts it: 'Our present condition, if we use it skillfully and with wisdom, can be an inspiration to free ourselves from the bondage of suffering'.[1]

Whilst karma is often viewed as purely an action–reaction chain, in Buddhism and especially in Western understanding, it is much wider than this. An ongoing, balancing process, karma is purposeful and can occur at any time. Edgar Cayce defined it as: 'the process by which we meet what we have created ... It is self that one has to meet. And what ye sow – mentally, spiritually, physically – that ye *will* eventually reap.'[2] Edgar Cayce was a deeply religious man and he often quoted, paraphrased or elaborated on the teachings of Jesus whilst in trance. The most often quoted teachings were: 'As you sow, so shall you reap,' and 'Do unto others as you would have others do unto you.' Cayce, on more than one occasion, gave a combination of the two: 'Be not deceived, be *not* deceived; do not misunderstand ... For what man sows, man reaps. Man constantly meets himself. Do good then, as He said, to those who have despite-fully used you; and you overcome then in yourself what you have done to your fellow man.'[3] In other words, in meeting your karma out there in the world, reflected back through the actions of others, you are offered an opportunity to clear your own karma through right action – a teaching also given by the Buddha.

So, for example, if a person is consistently generous to those around him, an ability which arises out of an inner sense of abundance, then over his lifetimes he will attract to himself generosity. People will treat him more magnanimously because he has been generous. On the other hand, if someone has always been suspicious of other people, mistrusting them and acting in a miserly fashion, then what he will have created is distrust. He will attract this distrust to himself and may well find himself accused by other people of being dishonest or find himself living in unalleviated poverty. Cayce emphasized many times that apparent misfortune is actually a tool for showing up our own shortcomings, offering an opportunity to redress what he called 'defects of character'.

What appears as accident or incident may well incorporate karma – and may be the trigger needed for change or karmic manifestation of a different kind. The path of karma is part of the evolutionary journey of the soul. Karma aids the soul in its learning and growth. It is neutral and impartial, neither 'good' nor 'bad'. It offers opportunities to overcome inherent weaknesses (deficits on the karmic credit card). It also affords the opportunity of utilizing the strengths and skills developed previously (the credits on the karmic credit card) and to concretize potential abilities.

Karma is an evolving future but it is powerfully affected by a person's beliefs. If someone views a karmic situation as an opportunity to learn, they will respond differently to someone who views it as karmic punishment or retribution. Although karma is neutral, its manifestation is often through difficult circumstances and, therefore, it may be perceived as 'bad karma' coming home to roost. This usually happens where people believe themselves to be victims of a fixed fate (the 'I can't help it, it's my karma' school of thought). Feeling helpless, they will make little effort to make the best of the situation or to change it. On the other hand, the same situation would be perceived differently by a person who sees karma as an opportunity to grow. Someone who views the same situation as a gift and an opportunity to learn will create a totally different – and, usually, much more positive – outcome from the same root cause. It all depends on the attitude of the soul involved and how the karmic situation is handled.

A couple whose child is born with a physical or mental impairment, for instance, may view this birth as a disaster. They may feel that 'God's punishment' is being inflicted on them – or on the child – and find it impossible to handle the resultant tensions. They will not necessarily seek out what is best for the child. Even when seeming to accept the situation, they could be ignoring its deeper meaning – and the opportunities it brings for personal and family development. Another couple might do all they could for the child, but want to turn the child into a 'perfect child' instead of accepting the child as already perfect in his or her own way. Such a couple would, most probably, be guided by 'experts' who told them what to do. This could involve abandoning the child 'to its fate' or trying to force the child to conform to the 'norm'. Yet another couple would do all they could to bring the best possible quality of life to that child, allowing the child's full potential to emerge whilst accepting and loving the child as he or she was, treasuring him or her as a unique individual. This couple would perhaps look at more unorthodox methods of helping the child and seek ways in which they themselves would grow through the situation. They would experience the child as a gift rather than a punishment.

A learning disability or physical impairment can be the incarnating soul's choice. The soul may be offering a gift to the parents so that they can grow, or it may be an experience the soul itself has decided to undertake. It is impossible to assess from the perspective of earth whether such a situation is retributive, regressive or growth-inducing. The impairment could be the result of lifetimes of ingrained attitudes or thought patterns, or a physical injury carrying forward from another life; or a seeming accident of birth. The same applies to many other situations. As Edgar Cayce, who worked extensively with karmic causes, pointed out: 'the weaknesses of the flesh are the scars of the soul' and many souls do incarnate to overcome or to make reparation for previous misdemeanours, actions or attitudes.

Karma is often viewed from the perspective of judgement and punishment. People are seen as being rewarded for past actions which were 'good' or being punished, or making reparation, for transgressions. In other words, karma is seen as the fate that shapes life and that underlies suffering. In this view, whatever a man, or woman, experiences is purely the product of previous behaviour. 'What a man sows, that shall he reap.'

So, for example, the deterministic view of karma says that someone who has put out another person's eye in a past life would be born blind in the next life as retribution. The person would, in that view, be said to be suffering from 'negative karma' which had to be paid back. However, karma is neutral. It is neither good nor bad. It simply is. Whilst one person may experience this 'boomerang' type of karma and be born blind or be blinded in an 'accident', it is equally likely that reparation could be made in another way. The person could become, for instance, an eye surgeon who saved many people's sight; or someone who donated their eyes for a corneal graft after their death. Notwithstanding, most people who are born or become blind will not be making karmic restitution. They could well be developing other senses and inner qualities through their experience, which will not be a form of punishment but rather a constructive path of soul growth.

Avoiding value judgements and not looking at karma from the perspective of 'past-action-equals-root-cause-and-inevitable-outcome' means that karma can be viewed as *something that happens and produces an action–reaction or result as part of an ongoing process.*' The Buddha said: 'What you are is what you have been, what you will be is what you do now,' whilst the Buddhist sage Padmasambhava expressed it: 'If you want to know your future life, look to your present actions.' What is set in motion now, will continue and project forward into the future – which means that a choice can be made deliberately to set in motion constructive potential for the future by changing thought patterns and having a positive attitude. The karma will still be neutral, but it can be taken advantage of constructively and will appear to be good karma manifesting.

Even when karma *seems* to be manifesting negatively, taking value judgements out of the equation can change the picture. For example, during a past-life regression, a woman discovered that an abortefactant, a substance which would cause a spontaneous abortion, had been administered to her in a past life, without her knowledge or consent. The resonance had stayed with her soul and had manifested as multiple sclerosis, as one of the ingredients had been a neurotoxin. The multiple sclerosis was not a punishment for the act of aborting the foetus (to which she had been an unwitting party) but it was a result of the past-life abortion. Her soul's consequent dis-ease manifested in her present life as a physical illness. During the regression session, she went into the between-life state and it became clear to her that her actions during her present life, how she handled and healed the dis-ease, would affect her next life. If she cleared the dis-ease, she would be born healthy. If she did not, then she would probably be born with neurological damage as the condition would become more ingrained.

> **Between-Life State**
> *Not all souls are instantly reborn into a physical*
> *body. Those who are not occupy a less dense*
> *'body' in a space not located on earth – although*
> *it may have a similar appearance. To the soul,*
> *this space is solid and tangible. It may be called*
> *Heaven or Hell, the Bardo, the Otherworld, the*
> *Afterlife, karmaloca and so on. Souls spend an*
> *indefinite period in this space until ready to*
> *return to earth.*

Karma is not just the result of direct action, it can also arise from attitudes, thoughts, desires and actions that have not been taken when perhaps they could have been. A thought is a powerful manifestor of karma, particularly if it arises from ingrained habit. Thought creates. The thoughts of yesterday are the physical reality of today. Someone who has an habitual attitude of resentment, for instance, can produce physical illness or circumstances for themselves which give them something tangible to resent. Last thoughts are particularly potent. A person who dies believing, 'There will never be enough,' is likely to be born again with the propensity for addiction or poverty.

What Carries the Karma?

What carries the karma depends on which lens karma is being viewed through. Viewed from the perspective of the Hindu or the Western believer in reincarnation, it is the *atman* or eternal soul. What Edgar Cayce called 'the eternal identity' and Rudolf Steiner 'eternal individuality'. This 'eternal identity' puts on different personalities or personas rather like an actor takes on roles which are played for a period of time and then put aside. The actor, however, remains essentially the same throughout although he may be so carried away by his role that he forgets, for a time, that he is only acting. In the same way, the soul can become so submerged in the present life, that it thinks that body is all there is – and in most traditions incarnating souls are in any case bathed in merciful forgetfulness so that they do not remember all that happened in other lives. Nevertheless, the karma carried by the soul manifests even though the cause is not remembered. The soul or eternal identity, however, carries a knowledge of all that has happened.

Another way of looking at the concept of the soul and its karma is to view each life as a bead which is strung together with others. The thread that holds them together is the soul, with the karma passing from the soul into the next life. However, this view emphasizes a linear progression and it is clear from regression experiences that linear time, once out of incarnation, has no meaning.

Through the lens of Buddhist belief, however, there is no eternal identity. At death the personality fragments and *skandhas* or separate parts carry a seed of karma into another existence but no individuality (see Chapter Eleven). Each seed can incarnate into a different 'new' person, each influenced by the karma of the past life. So, in the Buddhist view, karma is independent of soul.

> ## Skandhas
> *The fragments or constituents that bond together to create experience of life. They comprise: form (or body), feeling (or sensation), perception, intention and consciousness.*

Ongoing Process

Karma is continually being set in motion and working itself out. Karmic consequences may become apparent in five minutes, a week, in a year or two, or in another lifetime. As an ongoing process, karma can be changed, and is constantly evolving. Positive, constructive karma can be set in motion and reparation can be made to overcome negative karma.

Some schools of thought teach that everything has to be experienced. So the soul has to know sorrow and joy, pain and happiness, longing and fulfilment, male and female. It must be both murdered and murderer, warmonger and appeaser, rake and celibate. It will have incarnations that encompass all these extremes but little will be carried from life to life. The soul will simply experience the situation, and then move on. In another school of thought, rather than getting itself murdered, the soul of a murderer could become the parent of the soul it had murdered and thus learn to cherish that soul. Once karmic process is looked on as one of balance, 'fault' and judgement drop away. All is experienced because the experience is needed.

Balance is also created through fundamentally opposing attitudes to life arising in different incarnations. Someone who is now very introverted and sensitive, could well be balancing out lifetimes of extroverted egotism. Another soul who has led many lives as an aggressive male might choose to inhabit a female body, or could be a softer, intuitive male who might well choose relationships with other men rather than women – and thus be likely to experience a 'macho' man's aggressive reaction to the fear he feels when confronted with someone who is different to himself.

Karma may also be a test the soul sets for itself to see how well it has learned a lesson. So, for instance, someone might have had several very successful, outgoing lives. The challenge then could be to avoid selfishness and self-indulgence, learning to think of others. While things went well, he or she would be the life and soul of the party, optimistic and fun to be with. But, the soul asks, can this be kept up under very different circumstances? The test is arranged so that, at first, things go extremely well. The soul has the opportunity to develop a positive outlook once again. And then, seemingly, things go wrong. Bankruptcy is declared, a chronic illness develops, or a relationship ends. The challenge is to maintain that happy, positive, optimistic outlook despite the setbacks. To be able to be among people who have 'more than me' and yet not get bitter or resentful. A temptation may be to manipulate previous contacts or to put pressure on someone who 'owes me' so that things can 'get back to normal'. If illness sets in, attitudes may change. On the other hand, the soul might have decided it was time to put aside the outward-orientated approach to life and to develop introspection and inner-awareness. So, the loss of status, job, or whatever, could be designed to turn the soul inward to find different strengths.

Sometimes the greatest discoveries stem from small beginnings. Johannes Kepler (1571–1630) was a Renaissance astrologer, astronomer, mathematician and physicist. He recognized that the sun was the centre of our planetary system. His research led to an understanding of the dynamics of planetary motion and much else besides. In a preface to *De Harmonice Mundi (Harmonics of the World)* Kepler said:

> *Yes, it is I who have robbed the golden vessels*
> *of the Egyptians to make an offering to my God*
> *far removed from Egyptian bounds. If you will*

*forgive me, I will rejoice, but if you blame me I
must bear it; here I throw the dice and I write
this book. What matter if it is read today or later
– even if centuries must elapse before it is read!
God himself had to wait six thousand years for
the one who recognized his work.*[4]

Assuming that he is speaking literally rather than allegorically,
Kepler would appear to have had a glimpse of a life in an Egyptian
temple, possibly as an astronomer priest and probably as one
who served a 'different god'. Certainly Kepler's extensive study of
Pythagoras and Plato would have brought the concept of reincarnation to his attention. The indictment of Kepler's mother for
witchcraft might perhaps show why he hinted at his past-life memories rather than speaking openly of them. This was a period when
the Inquisition was hard at work rooting out 'heretics', and Kepler's
work sufficiently challenged the Roman Church and its established
notions of life to make it dangerous for him. Had his mother, whom
he himself defended at her trial, been found guilty, his official position as Mathematician of the Holy Roman Empire would have been
put in jeopardy. Had he openly confessed to memories of other lives
he would undoubtedly have received the unwelcome attentions of
the church. As it was, he was able to fulfil his karma and bring about
a revolutionary change in how the universe was viewed.

Fate and Free Will

Karma is often confused with fate. Fate means: 'It has been written.'
Religions such as Islam are based on submission to one's fate –
which has already been laid out by Allah. Many people who believe
in fate believe that life is as it is because that is what God decrees.

There is a fixed pattern laid down which cannot be deviated from. Viewed this way, fate is predestined and imposed by an outside force. It is what happens, there is no choice. It leaves no room for growth. In the eastern view, even *dharma*, or soul intention, is fixed in advance and the soul attains enlightenment by aligning to its *dharma* and overcoming its *karma*.

Fate offers no explanation as to *why* people suffer, other than 'this is what God wills' or 'this is what they deserve', or perhaps the medieval Christian belief that suffering has merit in its own right. Fate often seems capricious. It is vested upon someone. One of the best expositions of this kind of fate comes in the story of Job, recounted in the Old Testament.

Job inadvertently became part of a wager between God and Satan. God believed that Job was naturally god-fearing and would remain so whatever the circumstances. Satan surmised that it was because Job had, up until then, had a good life under God's protection. He told God: 'But, stretch out your hand and touch all that he has, and then he will curse you to your face.' (Job: 1:11)[5] God agreed that Satan could test out his theory, provided he did not take Job's life. Satan set out to make Job's life hell.

Job, seemingly, suffered because God decided he could suffer. After all, he had no idea that God and Satan had made an agreement about him – and there would have been nothing he could have done about it if he had known. Having lost most of his family and worldly goods, Job endured it because he felt it was his fate: 'The Lord gives and the Lord takes away; blessed be the name of the Lord', he declared. (Job 1:21) However, when inflicted with loathsome boils, even the interminably patient Job became angry with his God and cursed the day he was born saying: 'I will speak out in bitterness of soul. I will say to God, "Do not condemn me, but tell me the ground of thy complaint against me." '(Job: 10:2) God's reply is that, as Job cannot do any of the wondrous things God can do, God has the right to arrange Job's life in whatever fashion he wishes. A view that Job ultimately concurs with. He is happy to surrender to his fate.

Many people who believe in karma look on it as their fate. Fate implies, in the traditional, Hindu approach, that the soul is reaping penalties for past actions. Karma says: 'This is what has been earned.' Viewed fatalistically, that is that. Karma is 'cause and effect'. It is fate. It is what has been earned, karmically speaking, and it is not open to change. People who believe in this type of karma hold the fatalistic view that 'what will be, will be', and that the future is predestined. What will happen to them is fixed and unmoving, with no possibility of change or evolution unless this is part of the predestined life. So they see no point in trying to change things and extreme passivity sets in. The consequences of this belief are, as Gina Cerminara says: 'psychologically paralyzing and spiritually demoralizing'.[6] There is little point in striving to 'better oneself' or to overcome negative karmic circumstances if that is one's unyielding fate and so nothing is done to alleviate grinding poverty or disease.

There are times when rebirth does seem to be unplanned, with fate apparently holding sway. From information gained during regression sessions, some souls 'bounce back' into incarnation out of a strong desire to be in a physical body, or to be with a particular person, or because of something left unfinished. They may have made little progress in the spiritual world and 'hang around' the earth plane waiting to incarnate again. They have little choice in the matter, being ruled by their desires. They are pulled back by cravings, unfinished business, ingrained patterns, or vows that have not been rescinded. The major challenge for the present life may be to break the habits of lifetimes or to release someone – or oneself – from an outdated promise. It is these people who incarnate without plan or preparation who could be said to be 'fated'. A cause is having its effect.

But not everyone views karma fatalistically, and not everyone will experience karma and rebirth in this way. Whilst there are strong links between karma and fate, it is possible to believe in karma and still maintain that the soul is in a purposeful incarnation. Destiny is an evolving future whereas fate is firmly fixed and cannot be changed. The soul has a pattern that has been laid down – the fate or destiny as it were. But it also has free will. Free will is the power to change the future. It is the ability to grow and to find a positive outcome for karma. The incarnating soul can choose to encounter the result of its own handiwork or to make reparation for the past – no matter how hard a present life that may lead to. This can be a positive choice, both for the soul itself and for other people. The soul may take on collective karma, help someone else learn a lesson, and so on. Another soul may choose to take a path of grace and step outside the karma altogether, moving in a different direction from heretofore.

It is difficult to evaluate the long-term spiritual effects of traumatic or painful karmic experiences upon the eternal Self; the working of karma is, in any case, subtle and far from straightforward. Someone who may appear to be 'fated' because of trauma, illness or difficult life situations may have actually prepared most carefully for the incarnation and will have a profound reason for making that choice. It may be for personal growth and evolution, or to aid other people in their lessons or intentions. Belief in karma does not exclude chance or free will. Free will means: 'There is an opportunity to learn and grow.' Fate says: 'This is the future you have earned.' Free will says: 'Yes, but you have the ability to change it and create a new future.'

The key to karmic balance is in knowing when it is appropriate to submit to one's karma and when it is advantageous to break a cycle. In Hamlet's famous soliloquy Shakespeare has him ask:

> *To be, or not to be: that is the question*
> *Whether 'tis nobler in the mind to suffer*
> *The slings and arrows of outrageous fortune.*
> *Or to take arms against a sea of troubles,*
> *And by opposing end them?*

A deeply disturbed Hamlet is here deciding whether or not to commit suicide to end his troubles. That is, he hopes he will free himself from his fate. However, Hamlet is afraid that, even after death, those troubles will continue:

> *To sleep: perchance to dream: ay, there's the rub;*
> *For in that sleep of death what dreams may come*
> *When we have shuffled off this mortal coil,*
> *Must give us pause ...*
> *For who would bear the whips and scorns of time*
> *The pangs of dispiz'd love, the law's delay,*
> *The insolence of office, and the spurns*
> *That patient merit of the unworthy takes ...*
> *But that dread of something after death ...*
> *... puzzles the will,*
> *And makes us rather bear those ills we have,*
> *Than fly to others that we know not of?*

Elsewhere in his plays, Shakespeare speaks of reincarnation and he may well have known the doctrine of karma. He was certainly familiar with the dilemma of whether to follow one's fate blindly, or to exercise free will.

In the free will approach to karma, there are many ways of making reparation or restitution, if these are required. The murderer may achieve a degree of spiritual enlightenment and choose a life of service, for example. From the experiences of people who have near death experiences or who undertake past-life therapy, there are many ways of dealing with karmic debts. It does not appear to be mandatory to make direct repayment to the person who has been injured, although the choice may be made to do so. Once the incarnating soul has found someone to whom a similar debt is owed by another soul, to perform the appropriate task will be sufficient reparation. Neither does it seem to be necessary to fulfil every last duty or debt. The karma of grace operates. There is a point when enough has been done, understanding has been reached, and the soul is freed from the karmic round.

Rudolf Steiner discussed the question of free will and karma in a series of lectures he gave in 1910. He particularly addressed the situation where someone was healed by outside intervention of a condition which had arisen out of karmic necessity – that is, they were making reparation for a previous act. In Steiner's view, 'In a sick body there dwells a damaged soul which has come under a wrong influence.'[7] This soul was under what Steiner described as a 'luciferic element' but, in Steiner's view, that element could be overcome by love (a superior element). So, forms of healing that used love would be appropriate to support the damaged soul in finding resolution of the karmic imbalance that had been created. 'Because love is the fundamental essence of the soul, we may, indeed, influence the direction of karma,' Steiner concluded.[8] This 'love' and appropriate remedies obtained from the natural world underlie anthroposophical medicine.

There is, however, enormous debate, not only within anthroposophy and healing or therapy, about whether a healer (or anyone else) should intervene uninvited in someone else's karma. Some authorities believe that this directly contravenes a person's autonomy and free will; whilst others hold the view that if someone is able to help then it is their duty (or karma) to do so. My own teacher, the occultist and metaphysican Christine Hartley, held a middle view. Christine believed that an offer should be made, appropriate action taken if asked, but that the person should then be left to get on with things themselves unless further requests were made. If they refused help, that was their choice. If they accepted it, enough should be done but no more: 'You can help a lame dog over a stile,' she would say, 'but there is no obligation to carry him over the field as well. He will lose the use of his legs.' So, if she thought someone was requesting help in order to 'wriggle out of karma', she felt justified in saying no. If the person was not in a position to be consulted, say in the case of someone in a coma, then her advice was to ask that they would be healed 'if appropriate for their own highest good'.

The same advice applied to situations where, because of the person's beliefs, the offer would not be understood. For example, a young woman in my healing group asked for healing to be sent to her mother, a Roman Catholic in Ireland, who had had a heart attack. She knew that her mother regarded healing and the like as 'the devil's work' and yet, as a trainee healer, she felt that it was her karmic duty to help because she was 'aware of things that her mother had not yet discovered'. A healing circle was conducted for the mother, care being taken to ask that healing would be received in the way that was most appropriate for the mother. If it was her time to depart, then the healing would help her passing. If she could be healed, then it would aid that process. The next day there was a telephone call from Ireland: 'A miracle has happened!' The mother had recovered well. When the daughter, some time later, went back to Ireland, she told her mother about the healing circle. 'I always knew that you of all my children were special,' her mother told her. 'When I looked at you for the first time, I knew you.' Mother and daughter shared the opinion that there was a karmic bond between them, and that the daughter had become a healer so that she could help her mother and bring her to a new level of spiritual understanding.

In her karmic teaching, Christine Hartley stressed the difference between karma arising out of carrying out a duty and karma from volitional acts. In carrying out his 'duty', a person commits the act because he has to – unless of course he uses this as an excuse for his behaviour which goes beyond the call of that duty. So, for example, a state executioner was doing his work when he put someone to death and, provided he carried out his duties fairly and dispassionately, he would not accrue difficult karma (there would probably have been karmic reasons why he became the executioner in the first place). In the past, such a man would usually be appointed to the job with little choice in the matter – it could be an hereditary position, but it could be given at the whim of a ruler. But, if that man cruelly enjoyed his work, prolonging the agony for people, for example, then strong karma would accrue, as it would if he had applied for the position in the first place because he would enjoy the work.

Christine Hartley always used the example of war. To her, this was a manifestation of fate. If a man was caught up in a collective movement such as a war, then, in her eyes, it was his duty to fight for his country and no karma accrued. Other people would argue that everyone has a choice to make at this point and could become a conscientious objector or pacifist if they had a sufficiently strongly developed viewpoint. However, Christine stressed that it all depended on how a man dealt with his place in the greater scheme of things and the situation in which he found himself. If a soldier took pleasure in killing and if he tormented, tortured or raped whilst he was doing it, then considerable karma would result *even though he was conforming to the mores of his time*. It all depended on the attitude with which he met his 'fate'.

The concept of free will is one of growth and change on all levels. It is in direct antithesis to all those people who say: 'I can't help it, it's my karma.' This pathway says: 'You are responsible. Clean up your mess.' But it also says: 'You only have to do enough.' And, for some people, that 'enough' might include surrender to the guidance of divine will – which could well reverse the extreme wilfulness of a former life, for instance. The pathway of free will allows use of the skills, abilities and potentials brought to the current life, and healing for the wounds of the past.

However, it would appear that there are two karmic pathways – and maybe more. The first is that of free will and personal responsibility. The second is a surrender to divine will. Hindus and Buddhists believe that by submitting to their fate, as it were, and aligning themselves with divine purpose, they can move off the wheel of rebirth. The second pathway may be a genuine commitment to divine purpose. It all depends on how clear the alignment to divine will is – and how clearly the guidance from the Self or the divine is heard. Unfortunately, many people who believe they are following divine will are actually trapped in the patterns of the past. They re-enact the same old scenarios over and over again. Regardless of how cunningly disguised, abuse, for example, is abuse no matter whether it is perpetrated by a parent, a lover, or a guru under the guise of aligning to higher will and opening spirituality.

Lack of Personal Responsibility

The 'I can't help it, it's my karma' approach to life takes no responsibility either for having created situations that now need restitution, or for taking on tasks that may prove irksome. A person with this attitude will often blame those around him, or her, for the situation. They may also use the other person as an excuse for not doing something. So, the woman who says: 'I had to sacrifice my career to look after my husband and children' is not taking responsibility for her choice to marry and have children. The son who never leaves home or marries may well excuse himself with: 'Well my parents needed my financial support,' and a daughter may well use her ailing mother or father in the same way. This attitude can in itself create karma.

If someone has agreed in the between-life state to help someone learn a very difficult lesson; or to look after someone who, for their own karmic reasons, has to undertake illness or impairment, then it can lead to 'bondage' or freedom. If the person feels held back and blames the other person, they become tied to that person and they will find themselves together in another life. On the other hand, if someone can say: 'This is my choice. This is the way I want it to be,' they are free from karmic ties. Ruth White, who has worked extensively with karma, says: 'We are free of bondage only when we are able to make positive statements about limitations we've accepted.'[9] As she says: 'We should only make those sacrifices for which we take full responsibility.'

Accident or Design?

Just as not everything is attributable to karma, neither can every event be a matter of fate or free will. Collective karma outweighs personal karma, for instance, and people can get sucked into events. Accidents do occur and karma works at levels beyond the purely individual. A soul may belong to a soul group that has an agenda to deal with. It is clear from past-life regression and between-life testimony that not everything in a life is pre-planned, nor does everything necessarily go as envisaged. The environment may have its effect in the shape of chemical, functional or economic forces that intervene in life. The engine on an airliner is fouled by birds, for instance, causing the plane to crash and everyone to lose their life. 'Fate' or 'karmic causation' would suggest that everyone on that plane had carried out some action in the past that meant that they had 'earned' such a death. Chance, on the other hand, would suggest that it was mere happenstance that took each person onto that plane, just as it was pure chance that took the plane through a flock of birds at that particular time. Similarly, if a chemical or nuclear spillage affects hundreds of people, it could be termed accident rather than karma – although there may be some people caught up within that event who find their karma returning to them. Biological, social and racial factors may take their toll.

Few people would argue that everyone who died in the Holocaust, for example, was irresistibly attracted to that experience because of their individual karma. The Holocaust was part of a social movement and an ongoing racial experience of persecution. If karma was operating, then it was more likely to be at a racial or collective level. Nevertheless, there are occurrences which, from outside, appear to be random and yet the 'accident' or the event is exactly what the soul (or the race or collective) needs for the present stage of growth. So, for example, senior Tibetan lamas were told by their Oracle prior to the Chinese invasion of their country that this event would occur and drive them into exile so that they could take their teachings to the West which needed them. Since that time, an increasing number of lamas are reincarnating into Western bodies. Their faith is broadened by the experience, as are the souls whose lives they touch with their teachings. Buddhism is one of the fastest-growing philosophies in the West.

Karmic Inheritance

It is clear from the experiences of people who, in regression, enter the between-life state that a soul may choose to incarnate into a specific family which has a karmic inheritance that matches what the soul needs to undergo. This karmic inheritance may be genetic or concerned with race or privilege – or the lack of it. The inheritance may also be a talent or ability, or position, that is passed down through the family. It is also clear that, in some cases, a soul needs to experience a particular situation as reprisal or restitution for past actions and, therefore, incarnates into a family that has a specific karmic resonance.

In this latter instance, the experience may not be so much a matter of choice as a karmic necessity or compulsion. Such a karmic inheritance can be at a genetic or emotional level. So, for example, if someone needed to experience illnesses such as haemophilia or Huntington's disease or to suffer from alcoholism or addiction then they would incarnate into a family that carried the gene responsible for those conditions. This gene provides a 'seed potential'. Given the right karmic conditions, the seed matures.

Not everyone within the family, however, would manifest the condition for which the genetic potential existed because their karmic pattern may not fit the 'profile' required for the seed to germinate. It may be their karma to live in a family where some members have the condition and others do not, and, perhaps, to experience the uncertainty that such genetic issues can engender. They may need to make ethical choices such as whether, being a genetic carrier themselves, they should pass this on to their children in turn. Many other karmic issues arise in families with genetically transmitted diseases.

Skills and abilities often appear to travel through families. Musicians may be made with training, but they are often born with an in-built gift carried forward from other lives. However, they may need assistance to manifest their talent. It may not be scientifically provable, but there is such a thing as a 'musical ear' which is inherited. It has a particular shape, sounds have a certain resonance when received by it. So, if someone wants to be a musician, it would be wise for them to choose to incarnate in a family which has the genetic blueprint for the physical construction of such an ear. Similarly, they may need to inherit long, sensitive fingers rather than short, pudgy ones which will not have the right span to reach the notes. Careful planning allows karmic intention and ability to flower.

Nevertheless, there may be other reasons that someone chooses a particular family. It is not always a matter of heredity. The family may be ideal in other ways. Hypnotherapist Michael Newton reported a case of a man who, in the between-life state, explored his options for his next life. He decided that he would incarnate in New York and be a musician. However, he was trying to decide between two families. He thought that he would 'choose the dumpy kid with a lot of talent'. He commented that the body would not have the stamina that he had had in the life previous to that, but that he would have money. Saying that he knew that this sounded grasping and selfish, he explained that if he wanted to express the beauty of music and give pleasure to himself and others, then he needed proper training and supportive parents as otherwise, he was wise enough to know, he would get sidetracked.[10]

Biology and karma often interact. Edgar Cayce said on many occasions that the glands of the body conveyed karma (see Chapter Six). The propensity for the malfunctioning of certain organs or glands runs through families and may well create the 'breeding ground' for symbolic or attitudinal karma to flourish. So, for instance, a family which carried a history of heart diseases could allow a soul with a record of hard-heartedness to manifest that attitude physically.

Similarly, a soul may incarnate into a family with a long history of emotional or physical abuse. The soul would have the possibility of being abused or abuser, but could also avoid either condition. Abuse can arise out of a genetic propensity to conditions like alcoholism but may also stem from destructive emotional experiences. Violence, hatred and anger go together and endlessly recreate themselves. An abused child often becomes an abuser. Many abused children – and adults – confuse love with violence. They see violence as a way of showing 'love'. After all, it was the only attention they got, or the abuse brought on such an orgy of guilt in the abuser that they were then given considerable attention. If a soul has had difficulty in separating love and violence in the past, then it may incarnate again into an abusing family. However, if a soul wants to understand how abuse arises, it also may well choose to become an abuser or someone who is abused for the duration of one or more lives. Healing that abuse then becomes an option, as does forgiveness and the operation of the karma of grace.

An angry soul might be attracted by an abusive family as the opportunity is there for the playing out of that anger. Nevertheless, a soul who has accumulated much fear may also be drawn towards an abusing family. Its worst fears would be realized if it became the victim of violence – and this may be the way in which a soul chooses to overcome fear. On the other hand, someone who has been an abuser in other lives may need to experience how it feels to be abused. Karmic choices – or compulsions – are complex and difficult to assess.

'Inheritance' could also work more subtly to create karmic conditions for the soul's growth. A young woman 'inherited' a tendency to very painful and prolonged menses. This left her isolated as she often had to stay in bed and her mother worked long hours when her own health allowed. But the isolation, and the endocrine disturbance, allowed the young woman to develop her psychic abilities at an early age. Reading was a solace to her and through this she developed her own creative writing abilities. Both talents had commenced in other lives but were honed and put to use during her present life. She became a children's writer who incorporated spiritual and psychological understanding into her work. Her family background, which might to some eyes have appeared difficult, actually allowed her karmic purpose to flourish.

People are often attracted to families whose emotional make-up matches their own past patterns. So, someone who is angry but who rarely shows this could be pulled towards a passive–aggressive family where, outwardly, things are 'nice' but, under the surface, anger heaves and boils and is expressed in devious and, apparently, accidental ways. Another soul might have been attracted to that family because of the surface 'niceness' and then had to face the consequences of the hidden emotions. This soul might have been the 'people pleaser' in another life and then had to face the consequences of being 'nice' rather than authentic. 'Niceness' can be a most untrustworthy quality and one that creates considerable karma.

For some people, it is not so much a question of family and race as of place carrying the karmic inheritance. The earth has energies running through it and can carry the imprint of former events. There are minority groups, like the Druze of Southern Lebanon and Australian Aborigines, who believe they continually reincarnate within their own group or race. They carry not only their own individual karma but the collective karma of the group. This karma is continually being 'worked', each member of the group contributing to its continuation or its balancing out according to their actions in each life. They may also be carrying forward the group purpose.

Some people respond to the vibrations of a place. They may have unfinished business there or simply feel more comfortable in 'familiar' surroundings. T.E. Lawrence was never at home in England. He did not fit into his family or his society. The only time he enjoyed school was when he studied the Crusades and the military strategies involved. But when he went to Arabia it was a very different matter. He felt he had 'come home'. He became a military leader, said by some to be a genius. It is suggested by Gina Cerminara[11] that, in returning to Arabia, he was completing a life lived some time earlier as an Arab military strategist who died before his work was done. The place triggered his abilities and allowed him to flourish because, at a soul level, it was his home. Certainly, when Lawrence was forced to return to England, he became deeply depressed and soon died in an 'accident'.

The Karma of Place

Just as countries and races have their own karma, so too do places. Physical locations are powerfully affected by their karmic history. Sites of ancient battles or former sacred spaces in particular still carry an imprint of the events that took place there, although other places may well do the same. People who are sensitive to such things can pick up a psychic resonance regardless of how long ago they occurred. The spirits of those who should have passed on, or guardians of the land, may still remain in place. Karma of place can affect those who live there, whether or not they have set the karma in motion.

Dr Motoyama had a visit from a woman whose son had become schizophrenic and been hospitalized. Before hearing her story, Dr Motoyama had seen her enter his meditation centre, followed by a 'ghastly-looking warrior'. He saw that the tumuli in which the samurai had been buried had been defaced and scattered. The woman's father had bought the field in which it lay, and dug it up to make a paddy field. This act was quickly followed by a rise in the number of psychologically-disturbed people in the family and in the village nearby.

According to the woman's brother, the previous owners of the field had been known as 'the family of ruin' because anyone who bought anything from them ended up in trouble. Dr Motoyama prayed that the soul of the warrior would find rest. A week later, the woman's son was released from hospital, well enough to come home. Dr Motoyama was convinced that, at last, the spirit of the warrior had been relieved of his suffering.[12]

Taking over a site formerly consecrated to a different purpose can have karmic repercussions but other sites may carry 'good karma', with the people who settle there enjoying great prosperity or spiritual inspiration.

Group Redemptive Karma

Karma is not always clear and straightforward. There can be hidden agendas behind acts that would seem, on the surface, to attract karmic retribution. I recently regressed a woman to what turned out to be an attempt by a soul group to practise redemptive karma. In the former life, she was a young German soldier who was sent as a guard to a work camp. The young soldier was not at all happy about the job he was given, but he had no choice. He would have been shot had he refused. Eventually he was 'accidentally' killed during the liberation of the camp. We then went into the between-life state and there he joined many of the souls who had died in the camp. They were all, including the young man, despairing and angry, not because of what had transpired but because as he said: 'Our group chose to be involved as we thought that we could put a stop to atrocities because the world would be so shocked it would never allow such things to happen again. We sacrificed everything to try to turn the world away from acts like this. For a while it seemed as though we had succeeded. And yet we can see it occurring in the Balkans and in Afghanistan and elsewhere. Humanity appears to have learned nothing.'

FOUR

POSITIVE

Karma

Positive karma is often overlooked. It is as though people believe there can only be negative karma. They disregard the things they 'got right' in the past, and ignore the benefits and rewards they can reap from this in the present life – and do not realize they can create positive karma for the future. With all karma, there are credits and deficits. Positive karma is credit paid into the karmic piggy bank; it will stand the soul in good stead. Of course, acts of kindness, compassion and the like cannot be done on the basis of storing up positive karma for the future. That kind of motive will not create positive karma. Such a karma has to be unselfish, and the soul is often unaware of having clocked up the 'good karma' in the first place.

Recompense Karma

Recompense karma comes back, positively. Reward is given for sacrifices made to help others and for the things that the soul 'got right' in the past when learning a difficult lesson. Recompense is made for the suffering or deprivation that the soul underwent, provided that the soul experienced this with a positive attitude and did not succumb to an attack of the 'poor mes' or blamed someone else for its misfortunes.

So, for instance, if someone took time out to look after a partner who was ill or disabled and they saw this as an opportunity for serving that partner willingly and with love, then in another life they would be rewarded. If an ambition was put on hold to care for someone who was ill, the person who was looked after could well come back as a parent or good friend who helps out in the present incarnation. If someone experienced extreme poverty with equanimity, they would in another life enjoy abundance. If they bemoaned what they were missing out on, then there would be no recompense karma.

In recompense karma, the reward or restitution might come from the person who was helped in the other life, or from another source. Sometimes the recompense is for a very small act of kindness. In regression, one man went back to a life where he had given a cup of water to someone who was suffering extreme thirst. He did not know them in that life, but his compassion was great and he helped whenever he could. In his present life he had experienced great misfortune. Then one day someone offered him a chance to change his life. He took it eagerly and made a great success of things. But he always remembered his earlier misfortune and offered to others the same opportunity he had been given. To his surprise, during the regression, the person to whom he had given the cup of water was the man who had turned his life around. He felt that his 'small act of kindness' had been out of all proportion to what that man then did for him. But, as he saw when he looked deeper in the regression, that act had made an enormous difference. The thirsty man had died, he had been too far gone not to, but he had died following an act of loving kindness that made him resolve to help others in his next life.

In another scenario, a client was surprised to find that she went back to a very abusive life. She had had a terrible time as a slave. Owned body and soul, and much abused by her 'master', she endured it all stoically and with good humour. She never felt sorry for herself, she simply surrendered to the flow of life. As she had asked for the regression to find the basis of a very happy relationship and the former 'master' was her present lover, we went back to the between-life state before that incarnation. She found that she and the 'master' were part of the same soul group. The 'master' had felt a need to learn how it felt to abuse people, especially women, so that he could understand what motivated the abuser. She had volunteered to be the woman he abused so that he would not accrue karma for the future by that act. After her death, she forgave him and released him, offering him grace. As a result, when she was planning her present life, the man offered to be her life partner. She needed to experience a nurturing relationship and he felt a great soul love for her. Her recompense karma was repaid by a deeply loving relationship which was not rocked by difficult times. They were mutually supportive, bringing out the best in each other and finding ways to grow together.

Redemptive Karma

The urge to help humankind is an expression of redemptive karma. It is often associated with an act of self-sacrifice or martyrdom. Souls die so that their beliefs can come to wider attention, or so that others might live. Others make great personal sacrifices or take a stand to fight for a cause not for their own individual gain or glory but so that the lot of humanity, or their portion of it, will be improved. They may go on, despite setbacks or indifference, in the hope that what they have done will kindle a spark in someone else and that that person will be able to make the difference.

Some souls incarnate to help others or to do something specific for the world. High Tibetan Lamas, for instance, have usually had the opportunity to move off the wheel of rebirth several lives ago. But they come back to help others reach the same state. Disabled children may have chosen to come back to help their parents learn a lesson such as compassion and caring. The ultimate example of redemptive karma for Christians is when Jesus was crucified to 'take away the sins of the world'. However, other souls continue to take on

tasks that will help to clear collective karma. It is not always immediately obvious when redemptive karma is being practised and a
soul's situation can be easily misunderstood.

Redemptive karma may be a reaction to the past. Some souls, for
instance, having been caught up in wars, plagues, famines, etc,
develop a deep desire to do something to prevent such things occurring again. When they incarnate, they do so with the intention of
finding a way to alleviate the situation. In the recent historic past in
the West, this could well involve a vocation to enter a monastery or
convent so that the power of prayer could be used to change things.
In more modern times, this vocation may involve working within
the field of medicine or public health.

However, redemptive karma does not necessarily have any connection to a past life. A soul may see, in the between-life state, a
situation that needs aid. It may feel: 'This is where I can make a
difference.' That soul then incarnates with the specific intention of
helping humanity.

I was privileged to have a friend who died from aids (he felt that cap-
italization of the word gave too much power to the disease). At the
time, it did not occur to me that he was practising redemptive
karma. We did, after all, have somewhat different views on reincarnation and karma. He was not even sure there was such a thing
(although since his death he has communicated that he is now convinced). But looking back, recalling our conversations and reading
what he had written during the course of his life as well as talking
to people whose lives he had transformed through his healing work,
I would say that he was a powerful example of redemptive karma in
action. He wanted to do things for other people and he certainly
made a difference.

He worked in the field of personal development and healing for many years. Early on, he set up a charity which concentrated on healing work with hiv and aids patients. His group would go into hospitals to offer healing, and ran workshops to teach people with hiv how to stay healthy. He explored complementary medicine and used this to great effect. When he himself was diagnosed as having full-blown aids he used his techniques of positive thought combined with complementary therapies to support conventional treatment. He took part in drug trials so that 'other people could benefit', but there was no suggestion of martyrdom about this act, it was all part of his positive approach to life. He lived way past the normal life expectancy of people with aids, due in no small measure to the support and help of his partner. He overcame major illnesses such as cancer not once but several times. In the process he introduced his consultant to 'alternative treatments', which were incorporated into the hospital protocols. He lectured to medical students and was an inspiration to many people. No-one who attended the healing workshops he ran with his partner could believe that he was ill. He was a man who 'walked his talk'.

Eventually he contracted a virus that would destroy the oldest part of his brain where the instincts lurk and autonomous processes of the body are controlled, including speech and hearing. (An interesting part of the karmic process as old patterns would not then be carried forward after death.) He was offered, but declined, treatment that was highly toxic. He rang me to say it was time to move on to the next great adventure. I spent two and a half weeks with him as he was dying. It was an enormous privilege and contributed in no small way to my own spiritual growth. During that time he showed no fear. His thoughts were for his family and friends, and for his own spiritual progress. He said and did exactly what each needed to help them come to terms with death – and later proved to them all his continuing existence after his physical death.

Many people have seen aids as a punishment vested by a wrathful God upon people who commit 'unnatural acts' – a judgement which takes little account of the millions of people in Africa and the Far East who have contracted the disease through conventional sexual contact. I have a different perspective. To me, aids is an opportunity to develop love. The relationship between my friend and his partner, and between other people I have known with aids, was something special. The level of caring and the loving is extraordinary. This is especially so as hiv and aids can be such an isolating condition. Which was why, when I read Rudolf Steiner on the karmic causes of smallpox, a much larger picture suddenly opened up.

It is Steiner's belief that epidemics are opportunities to make reparation for previous karma. He also felt (at the start of the 20th century) that man's efforts to 'clean up' and wipe out diseases actually prevented people from creating the right conditions for karmic clearing. He points out: 'If karmic reparation is escaped in one direction, it will have to be sought in another. When we abolish certain influences, we merely create the necessity of seeking other opportunities and influences.'[1] It is his assertion that smallpox is one of the means of karmic clearing. It is an 'organ of unlovingness'. That is, people who have in other lives created unlovingness, will use smallpox to clear it. But if the disease, smallpox, is removed, then a new means will have to be found to karmically work out an antidote to unlovingness.

At the start of the 21st century, we are in a situation where smallpox has all but been wiped out in the natural environment (it exists in laboratories and may yet be used in biological warfare or set free again through an 'accidental' escape). But we have an aids epidemic sweeping the third world and the possibility of it becoming global. In England and the States, the fastest growing section of the population with hiv are women who are infected by their partner. Yet little is, so far, heard in the West either about how rampant the disease is in Africa, or how it is spreading through the heterosexual community in the West. One theory on how the aids virus arose is that it came from contaminated smallpox vaccine. In other words, one illness or symptom of karmic disease mutated into another.

When we look at the passionate hatred and isolation that some aids sufferers have experienced and the unique care and concern offered to others, we can see that this condition could well be an 'organ of unlovingness' or an opportunity to express and experience love. In this respect, it may well be that those who are infected are actually undertaking a mass act of redemptive karma.

Merit Karma

Merit karma is a reward for things the soul 'got right' in other lives, the lessons learned, the insights put into practice. It is money in the karmic piggy bank. Merit karma may be the reason why someone has a smooth and easy life – or receives help as and when it is needed. It often manifests as a talent in the present life. So, a musician can carry that ability over into the next lifetime, to become an infant prodigy or a natural musician. Equally, a soul may have learnt how to manifest abundance and to trust in divine providence. It will return as someone who can always find a way to make money, or who is naturally 'lucky'. Merit karma also operates on a more spiritual level, bringing an incarnated soul into situations where it will continue with previous spiritual progression, attracting the right teacher at the apposite moment, and so on.

Positive Attitudinal Karma

A positive attitude, such as a loving nature, optimism or innate trust, brought forward from another life, will create positive effects in the present life. Health, wealth and wisdom arise out of positive attitudinal karma. If someone has been open-hearted, generous and giving in the past they will have engendered a healthy heart and will attract to themselves abundance and joy. Even when life is difficult, someone with a positive attitude will flourish. They know how to turn things to their advantage, how to be content with what they have, and how to make the most of each day or whatever is appropriate to the circumstances they find themselves in.

As karma shows that we create our own reality, 'good karma' can be created within the present life to sow seeds for a good rebirth.

Abundance

There are many people in incarnation who have learnt the secret of abundance. They have developed the power of positive thought and creative visualization. They trust that the universe will meet their needs and hold a strong intention that this will be so. In some cases this has been taught as a specific lesson – the temples of Egypt had such a concept as did Jesus when he said: 'Consider the lilies of the field, how they grow; they toil not, they neither spin: And yet I say unto you, that even Solomon in all his glory was not arrayed like one of these.' (Matthew 6:28) Jesus goes on to reassure the believer that his 'father in heaven' will provide for him if he ceases to worry about tomorrow. In other cases, the soul has learnt through the course of many lives to create the right conditions for abundance to thrive. However it has been learned, abundance is one of the most positive of all karmic gifts.

Karma in Suspension

As not all karma can be dealt with at once, some of it remains in suspension to be dealt with at another time – which may or may not occur during the present life depending on how other factors progress. Whilst not all of this karma will be positive, a considerable amount of it may well be. If the soul makes a leap forward, clearing or balancing previous karma, then it could well be in a position to make use of previous merit or positive attitudinal karma which had been 'waiting in the wings' as it were.

Creating Positive Karma
for the Future

In *The Last Days of Socrates*, Plato has the great philosopher offer his advice for ensuring a good future for the soul. He says that a man 'must abandon bodily pleasures and adornments as foreign to his purpose and likely to do more harm than good.' If this man 'has devoted himself to the pleasures of acquiring knowledge; and so by decking his soul not with a borrowed beauty but with its own – with self-control, and goodness, and courage, and liberality, and truth – [he] has fitted himself to await his journey to the next world.'[2] A Buddhist then, and now, would recognize this teaching as one that could bring enlightenment and liberation from the wheel of rebirth. Freedom from desire and the cultivation of positive qualities are universally agreed to lead at the very least to a good rebirth and at best to cessation of reincarnation.

Although karma and reincarnation do not usually feature in Islam, the Bektashi Sufi sect accept rebirth, especially into animals. Their founder Haci Bektas Veli lived during the thirteenth century. Amongst his teachings were several intended to guide the soul to live a good life and to create a positive future:

> *Even if you are hurt, don't hurt others*
> *Be master of your deeds, words and passions*
> *that none may be harmed by them*
> *The foundation of spiritual awareness is*
> *respect for others*
> *The beauty of a man's soul is reflected in*
> *his speech*
> *Never demand from others what you find*
> *hard to give yourself*
> *Vilify no person and no people*
> *Only true learning leads the way from darkness*
> *Blessed are those whose lights dispel dark thoughts*
> *Never forget that even your enemy is human too*[3]

Tibetan Buddhists would add to this the practice of compassion for others. Unselfishness and small acts of kindness accumulate into a huge reserve of merit karma. Giving to others creates future abundance. When Jesus said: 'Do as you would be done by', he was giving practical advice for a meritorious future.

FIVE

THE KARMA
of Suffering

The rationale behind suffering has occupied men's minds for thousands of years. It is a question that most religions seek to answer. Why, if God is good and loving as most religions teach, do people suffer so much, seemingly without cause? The question of suffering was one which particularly struck the young Prince Siddhartha, who would later be known as the Buddha.

The prince had been protected from the world by his parents. He lived in a beautiful palace, had a lovely wife and wanted for nothing. Having never left the seclusion of his blissful existence in the palace, he became curious about the outside world. Eluding his guards, he went with a servant to explore the world beyond the walls. Here, in the teeming mass of people, three things stood out for him: an old man, a sick man, and a dead man. Things he had never seen before. Asking his servant why these people should suffer so, he received the reply that such things were not uncommon, this was the lot of humankind. The prince was so moved by this that he renounced all his possessions and set out to find the cause of suffering. Years later, he formulated the reasons for suffering and a path of liberation from that suffering. These reasons included and went beyond karma.

Karma does, in many respects, explain suffering. If what is set up in one life has consequences in the next, then suffering may be retribution, reparation, or a way of learning what it feels like to experience certain situations. Tibetan Buddhists say that suffering is a broom that sweeps away 'negative karma'. It can, however, also reflect a state of inner dis-ease. If a soul has become out of harmony with karmic purpose, has lost sight of its divine roots, and feels alienated and cut off, then suffering will arise. One definition of suffering is 'isolation from God', although some religions see suffering as a way of gaining God's favour. If a soul suffers enough, it must ultimately be rewarded, or so the argument goes. In this view, suffering has merit in its own right. Nevertheless, it is clear from regression work and from the insights gained by psychics, that some souls become stuck in suffering. It may be addictive. It is what a Christian friend of mine describes as being 'stuck at the foot of the cross' rather than truly understanding the meaning of the resurrection. The soul wallows in its suffering, getting immense satisfaction from the depth of that suffering. It can take considerable work to raise such a soul from the ingrained habit – the antidote is often sought in 'ministering to the suffering' where a kind of vicarious suffering goes on, so little karmic progress is made.

Astrologer Alan Candlish defines suffering as 'the pain we experience as a result of [our] own guilt, fear or ignorance' and asserts that: 'used positively, however, suffering helps to strengthen and purify the individual.'[1] He separates the overall principle of suffering into 'suffering', 'non-suffering' and 'unsuffering'. Non-suffering involves coming to terms with individual suffering, and putting the insights gained to work to help heal oneself and others. It also requires giving up ego and self (with a small 's' as opposed to Self which is the divine principle). Unsuffering involves 'surrendering ourselves entirely to creation (God)'. In this way the soul aligns to its higher nature. It offers the opportunity of 'becoming that which we truly are, acknowledging and utilizing the gifts that are our own and bringing the healing light of love into the world'.[2]

In Tibetan Buddhism, suffering is said to arise out of selfishness, but according to Sogyal Rinpoche its karmic purpose is to awaken compassion. Nevertheless, in Tibetan eyes, suffering results from selfishness. A Tibetan sage, Shantideva expressed it:

Whatever joy there is in this world
All comes from desiring others to be happy,
And whatever suffering there is in this world
All comes from desiring myself to be happy.[3]

Awakening Compassion

The positive side of the experience, and the karmic purpose behind suffering, is to awaken compassion in the soul. For this reason, from regression work, it is clear that many souls choose to suffer not as some kind of retribution but as a way of opening to compassion – compassion for oneself and for others. People who take on redemptive karma often suffer in order to 'remove something from the world' as several cancer patients have expressed it. Mac in Chapter Seven used the Tibetan practice of *Tonglen*, taking the suffering of others into himself and using his death to transmute it on their behalf so that it could be cleared (see Chapter Eleven).

Suffering and Unconditional Love

Suffering also helps to awaken unconditional love. It can be extremely difficult to stand by placidly whilst someone suffers and yet that may be exactly what is needed. If the soul took on the suffering for a specific purpose, what may be required is the unconditional love and support to go through that process *whatever it entails*. Similarly, if the suffering is an act of retribution or reparation then it offers an opportunity to practise unconditional love – which accepts a person as they are and honours that person's innate right to be that way.

WAY of

> **Unconditional Love**
>
> *Loving and accepting someone as they are, with all their failings and foibles; seeing what they could be, and yet honouring what they are in the present moment. Unconditional love does not force change, neither does it oblige the person practising unconditional love to be misused in any way. It sets boundaries whilst allowing the other person to be what they are.*

There are some people, however, who cope with what other people would see as suffering without considering it so. A blind man travelled many miles to attend one of my workshops. He was asked, somewhat coyly, by a woman, what he thought he had done to deserve his blindness. He replied that he thought he had made a deliberate choice to take on blindness as a learning experience. It had opened him to so many things and taught him independence. The woman, however, had clearly seen his blindness as a form of boomerang karma. But he certainly did not 'suffer' from it nor did he see it as a form of retribution. An old Indian wise saying goes:

> *Who is blind?*
> *The man that cannot see another world.*
> *Who is dumb?*
> *The man that cannot say a kind word at*
> *the right time.*
> *Who is poor?*
> *The man plagued with too strong desires.*
> *Who is rich?*
> *The man whose heart is contented.*

Boomerang Karma

According to most sources on karma, boomerang karma underlies a great deal of suffering. In my own practice, I have seen little evidence of this unless the soul had refused to listen to 'wake up calls' over several incarnations. Boomerang karma occurs when something a person previously did to someone else happens to them. 'A harmful action directed towards another person seems to rebound on the perpetrator of the action.'[4] For example, a person having an angry thought about another person and wishing them harm may well stub a toe or knock into a door, seemingly accidentally. This is 'instant boomerang karma'.

In the longer term, that thought or action may have occurred in another life but the manifestation is in the present. An act in one life is mirrored by a condition in the present. Edgar Cayce gave many instances of this in his work. He read for an American professor, born blind, whom Cayce saw, in a Persian incarnation, as a member of a tribe who blinded its enemies with red-hot irons. The professor had been the officer who carried out the blinding.[5] It was one of the responsibilities of his position. Had he not carried out the task, he would have been punished. Gina Cerminara, who reported this case raises the question, 'How can an individual be held morally responsible for a duty imposed on him by the customs of the society in which he lives?' This is a difficult area *if karma is looked on as punishment*. If it is regarded as impersonal, divine justice balancing out former actions, then the perspective changes. The man is born blind. He experiences what it feels like to be blind, to have no sight. But he does not go through exactly what his victims experienced – the agony of the process of being blinded. Possibly, had he been a man who enjoyed his work and derived sadistic pleasure from the blinding, then he could have been born with sight, had a painful accident and then experienced the agony his victims went through. But he didn't. He is experiencing exactly the same affliction that he created in others.

In this case, there was no suggestion that the man's parents had been among his former victims. It is often assumed that boomerang karma is a kind of 'tit for tat' karma in which one person has something done to him, and then turns around and does it to the person who did it to him. Having examined all the Cayce readings, however, Gina Cerminara found no case in which the victim in one life became the perpetrator in another: 'In no case in the Cayce files was the present-life affliction found to have been instigated by the former victim of the person in question'.[6]

In regression, I have found instances where this reversal of the roles occurred, but it was usually accidental or incidental rather than deliberately inflicted and was frequently accompanied by a vow on the part of the person who was 'victim' the first time to 'get even' or to 'get my own back'. In other situations, great resentment arose *and was held onto past death*. It seems as though, if the situation is resolved within one life, then the personal interplay does not carry over. Only when the animosity is very strong or when the people concerned were in close relationship do they come back together to replay the scenario with different roles. In such situations, forgiveness is called for – and indeed such an interaction could well form part of a karmic theme running through several lives (see Chapter Three).

Retributive Karma

Retributive karma is similar to boomerang karma but it does have the feel about it of retaliation for former actions. In severe cases it may also incorporate an element of punishment and retribution. For example, if someone chopped off another person's leg in a former life, they could have a withered limb in the present life, or become crippled in some way. Disembowelling someone could lead to gut problems in the present life. In other words, what is done to others comes back with a recognizable connection between cause and effect.

The working out of this karma rarely occurs between the two people who were involved in the original action in the previous life – except where it is a case of revenge or a similar scenario. Retributive karma is often a 'wake up call' engineered by the higher reaches of the soul. It can lead to 'soul awakening'. In cases where the soul has failed to learn a lesson after many experiences, karmic justice may be served by a person, perhaps from the soul group, acting as the instrument of 'divine retribution'. The aim, however, is to turn the soul towards a different way of being, to free it from a habit pattern that has become ingrained.

Retributive karma can occur on several levels. It can be physical, as in the case of a withered or amputated limb. Or, if a person has consistently overeaten, then gut problems may result. It may also be mental or emotional. Someone who created profound mental disturbance in someone else, may find that psychiatric illness results in the present life; another person may have been cold and unloving in the past, and find him- or herself isolated and alone in the present. However, the field of influence can be wider than this. The effects may be felt in the environment, social or external.

Gina Cerminara reports that, in the Cayce files, there are numerous examples where someone, for example, wantonly destroyed forests or mined for minerals, irreparably damaging the earth. The karma would rebound through similar resources. One of my clients relived a past life where he destroyed vast tracts of land in the 'Badlands' of America, in a greedy bid to grow 'more and more'. His enterprise failed, however, due to a drought. He had turned to organic gardening in his present life, but found it unproductive financially. After the regression, he felt 'the slate has been wiped clean.' His business thrived and he began to enjoy financial rewards.

Another man had an example of family karma which interwove with retributive karma. His great grandfather made his money in the South African goldfields. He prudently invested the money in houses which were rented out. These houses passed down the family. By the time this man inherited them, they were badly in need of repair and had become something of a slum. He failed to make the repairs but enjoyed the extra prosperity that the rents brought him. Eventually the council ordered the houses demolished. The man received very little compensation. What he did receive, he invested in silver at a time when prices were rocketing. When they fell suddenly, he lost his money. Ironically, he worked as a solicitor and his main work was in preparing tenancy agreements which were heavily weighted in favour of the landlord. After his experience, he turned to representing a group of people whose houses were to be demolished to make way for a motorway. He fought for better compensation for them. Although he was not aware that he was clearing his karma at the time, it was an excellent way of 'balancing the books'.

Symbolic Karma

In symbolic karma, the present-life condition symbolizes what was done or how a person felt in the past. It can be a form of allegory.

A witch-ducker in a former life incarnated again as a bed-wetter, for example. A man who had 'shed much blood' in the past suffered from anaemia in his present life. In the same way, someone who misused communication in the past, could incarnate with a speech or hearing defect. Edgar Cayce told one client who had a hearing problem: 'Never again close your ears to cries for aid.'

Symbolic karma can, however, work in another way. There is something called 'organ language' in which anxieties and emotional conditions are reflected through psychosomatic dis-ease. If someone loses their appetite, they could well be emotionally starved. If the condition is not rectified, anorexia nervosa could result. A person who has difficulty swallowing, for example, or who experiences persistent nausea may not be able to stomach something, either in the present environment or from another life. This may relate to an attitude held, or an act committed by someone else, it may be feelings and emotions in the person concerned, or words that cannot be expressed.

I have a good friend, an American who suffered from 'gas'. She continually felt like there was a bubble burning in her oesophagus which she could neither swallow nor expel. In a workshop, she went back to a life where she was handed a poisoned drink. As it went down, it burned her gullet. But what hurt worst was that it was handed to her by her lover. She felt betrayed and that was something she 'could not stomach'. When she reported back, I asked her if she had thought to drink the antidote. 'No,' she said, 'I was too mad. To think, I had been taken in by him!' She went back into the regression and took the antidote, but she had a great deal of work to do later to forgive both the lover and herself for having been duped. However, the gas went away and did not return.

Symbolic karma may well underlie dis-ease. Feelings of guilt, for example, can be 'acted out' in the body and the resultant organic imbalance will reflect the previous life situation (see Chapter Seven).

'Sins of Omission and Commission'

The *Book of Common Prayer* of the Church of England defines the sins of omission and commission as: 'those things that have been done that ought not to have been done, and the things that have not been done that should have been done.' Omission means non-action, commission action. These 'sins' or 'separations from God' create karma and it is not just acts that have consequences. Not taking action can have as much karma attached to it as taking action – if the action or non-action is ill-advised it can create suffering.

If a soul always behaved in a certain way, or consistently refused to take action, or to learn a lesson, then the karma comes around and around until the message is understood. Lives can be experienced as 'sinning' or 'sinned against' as the soul struggles to find a way out of the repeating pattern. Greed, avarice, lust and the like are experienced over and over again, but so is the inability to move beyond something known and comfortable. The soul's failure to take a risk can accrue karma just as strongly as the soul who takes an unwise risk and fails.

So, for instance, a man may grow up in conditions of affluence but fail to share his wealth with those who live in less fortunate circumstances. This is a 'sin of omission'. What he did not do could no doubt lead to his experiencing privation in another life so that he could learn what it was like to live under such conditions. If he had achieved his wealth by the exploitation of others, rather than inheriting it or making the money 'honestly', then he would have committed a 'sin of commission' and could well find himself in a life where he in turn was exploited. On the other hand, he may find himself yet again in a life of ease and plenty if his soul wanted him to learn the lesson of altruism and gratitude.

Negative Attitudinal Karma

Negative attitudinal karma arises out of a characteristic approach to life: a stance or fixed opinion which is slavishly followed. The attitude is most often held regarding relationships, another race or religion. It is usually based on bigotry, indoctrination, ignorance, hatred or fear. The karma may be a repeating pattern with an ingrained attitude carried from life to life. For instance, someone who is cruel and hard-hearted may well have several incarnations where an inflexible, cold attitude to others is displayed. (Attitudinal karma frequently leads to dis-ease, see Chapter Seven.)

Some negative attitudinal karma, however, arises out of how someone was treated in a past life. A person who was abandoned by a partner, for instance, may have problems with commitment in the present life, becoming a 'commitment phobic' who fears intimacy. The resultant attitude is one of holding back, never giving of oneself in a relationship. A similar attitude can arise out of a love affair which ended badly, or unrequited love. If, in a previous incarnation, a woman found out that her husband had been unfaithful, in her present incarnation she could well carry an attitude of unreasonable and unfounded jealousy which would make itself known whenever her present-life husband spoke to another woman. Many such attitudes towards 'love' arise out of previous experience.

Attitudinal karma often arises out of religious beliefs. How people were involved in religion can have a profound effect on their attitude to it in the present life. Whilst some people carry-over deep religious conviction, and sometimes religious intolerance or fanaticism, other people may go to the opposite of what they knew 'back then'. A woman who had been in a convent in several incarnations, came into her present incarnation determined to make up for all the 'good times' she had missed. Her attitude was 'more, more, more' and she took to drink and sex in a big way. A Cayce illustration of how a present-life attitude to religion arose out of the past was that of a newspaper columnist who was extremely sceptical where religion was concerned. According to Cayce, he had been a Crusader in a former life who became thoroughly disillusioned when he witnessed the gap between what was professed as religion and the barbarities practised by its adherents on the Crusade. His deep-seated distrust of religion passed into his current life.

Some attitudes are persistent and can have violent consequences. These relate especially to a hatred for anyone who is 'different'. Edgar Cayce read for an Alabama farmer who founded a Society for the Supremacy of the White Race. The farmer hated black people with a particular intensity described as 'fierce and unrelenting venom'.[7] According to Cayce, in a past life he had been a soldier who was taken prisoner by Hannibal and sent to the galley of a slave ship. The overseers, who were 'coloured', treated him cruelly. One of them beat him to death. His fierce hatred passed into his present life, spanning three other lifetimes and twenty-two centuries. His present-life attitude caused considerable suffering to others. It remains to be seen what the karmic outcome of his ingrained attitudes will have on his future lives. It seems likely that he could ultimately create for himself an unhealthy body or incarnate into one of the races he has so much despised.

Attitudinal karma can subtly mould a personality towards suffering. The attitudes a soul holds can, of course, change over the course of several lives and there is typically a pattern of, for example, sociability or isolation running through lives as the soul first projects itself out to the world and then turns inward to examine itself. So, a soul could have a 'laissez faire' attitude to life: easy come, easy go. Incarnations would be passive but sociable. This soul would probably take on few serious responsibilities but would help out a friend in need. Then an incident could occur that would change this pattern. Say in one incarnation the person had a serious injury. If the response was still placid, little would change. Some introspection might be forced upon the soul in long hours of inactivity, but the soul might fill these with visits from friends. But if the soul saw itself as victim and asked: 'Why would this happen to me', it could lead to becoming embittered and isolated. The next life would then carry a different attitude, one of self-preoccupation or self-centredness. Such a person is unlikely to be sociable and so isolation would result and, most probably, self-pity or arrogance.

An 'ivory tower' attitude can arise where all the soul thinks about is itself and what it needs. On the other hand, it may spend all its time feeling sorry for itself. In the karma created through 'sins of omission' as far as its fellow human beings are concerned, the soul could then no doubt attract a very difficult life in an effort to balance out the karma. At some point, the soul would realize that it had to look within for the cause of this discomfort. Having done this, it would then manifest lives where it could expand once more into a social being with positive attitudes. Then the test comes. Can those attitudes be maintained in the face of suffering and adversity? If there is a trace of the 'poor me' attitude left, the answer is probably no. If the lesson has been learned, then the soul holds to its positive attitudes and either overcomes or accepts with good grace the situation in which it finds itself.

The Karmic Treadmill

It is clear from regression work that some souls are too passive to break out of a cycle of suffering. They go on suffering because they feel there is some vicarious merit to be gained from it; or they do not take opportunities to change their life, either through fear or a sense of inadequacy. I worked with a man who developed the ear condition tinnitus when his wife died. This became his unconscious excuse for not socializing with people. He became isolated and said that he wanted things to change. However, when hands-on healing brought him to a situation where he could hear again, it became clear that he could not cope with what seemed to him the enormous burden of starting up a conversation. Prior to his wife's death she had been the outgoing part of the couple. He had been content to sit and listen. He stopped coming for healing.

Some time later, he decided to try again. We looked at his past lives to see what lay behind his difficulty in communication. We found life after life where he had been isolated and withdrawn – from choice, he 'liked it better that way'. He had set up a treadmill of non-communication and loneliness which was comforting in its familiarity. In his present life, he and his partner had come together to help him get over this pattern. In socializing with his wife, he had learnt to enjoy other people's company, although he rarely had much to say as he was afraid people would think he had little to contribute. His wife's death had been a 'wake up call', a point where he could either relapse into the old pattern or move forward. Once he understood how he had been on a karmic treadmill, he began to venture out. Picking up the threads of his old social life, he was surprised to find people had missed him. This gave him confidence to go forward.

Other souls experience the karmic treadmill because it is what they have come to expect. They have had several lives where a certain situation or condition prevailed, and they come to believe 'this is how it will always be.' Until they change that expectation, that is how it is.

Destructive patterns that have not been outgrown go round and round. The soul is stuck in a groove. Many kinds of suffering are related to the karmic treadmill. Alcoholism is one example, relationships can provide many. If a soul believes: 'There will never be enough love', or 'I don't deserve to be loved', it will manifest relationships where there is no love. The expectation is reinforced, and round the soul goes again. Not only that, children will most probably inherit the attitude so that it multiplies and carries on down through the family.

Many people experience karma as an endlessly repeating cycle. This is because of deeply ingrained reactive patterns that have arisen over many lifetimes. The soul goes over and over the same old ground, unable to move forward. So, a soul may become stuck in a feeling of unworthiness – and will attract many situations that, apparently, confirm that unworthiness. The soul will look to others for support, seeking worth through their eyes rather than finding it within itself. The pattern will be reiterated life after life until the soul can break out of the bondage of unworthiness and learn to recognize its own innate value.

The 'groove-type' pattern frequently occurs in relationships where two souls, or whole families, incarnate together again and again, despite the fact that they have long ago learned everything they had to learn from each other, and had repaid any karmic debts they had. They return together from habit. At some point, they have to learn to let go of each other and move on.

There can be the 'swinging pendulum' pattern where in one life an extreme is lived out and then in the next the opposite extreme, and then back to the first and so on. The pendulum can swing between the spendthrift and the miser, for instance. At some point the soul must learn how to be able to both spend and save money instead of swinging wildly between the two extremes.

The pendulum can also happen, for example, when a man or woman indulges in irresponsible, promiscuous behaviour, often finding it impossible to commit to one partner. There may be many affairs outside marriage, or the soul simply moves from person to person using them to gratify sexual desire but giving nothing in return. Then, in the next life, the soul may strive for celibacy or may tie itself to an unsuitable partner for life, perhaps as a result of a momentary whim or 'lapse'. A child may result who suffers because he or she is aware that there is no love between the parents and who feels him- or herself to be an encumbrance without which the parent could be free. The unfinished business of karma may be to find a new way of responding to situations.

In this example, the soul might have to learn commitment with discrimination, perhaps having to go through a relationship which has to be recognized as unsuitable and then let go of, before moving on to the next partner. If the same child has reincarnated within the relationship (a frequent occurrence), then the task is to find a way to be loving and responsible to that child without necessarily staying with the other parent.

The unfinished business of a relationship pattern is often concerned with one soul taking responsibility for itself; giving up responsibility for someone else; or learning to be independent. Co-dependence is a common pattern in which the soul feels it will die without the other person. Similar patterns include saviour–rescuer and victim–martyr, or persecutor and persecuted scenarios in which one soul can always take the dominant role or the partners can alternate roles. Walking away from the situation can be an enormous challenge but may be the only solution to the recurring motif.

Other types of karma can underlie suffering but these are dealt with in the next chapter as they are contributors to the soul's dis-ease.

SIX

THE KARMA
of Dis-ease

Most commentators and teachers on karma see illness either as being caused by 'evil deeds' in a former life or by dis-ease of the soul. The dis-ease may be an imbalance, a reaction or a deficit that 'has to be rectified'. It can be symbolic of a former attitude, intent or action. It may even arise out of ill-wishing or an intentional curse. To Rudolf Steiner, for example, a weak constitution could be traced back to egotism in a former life. This would create dis-ease at an inner level and could manifest physically, emotionally, mentally or spiritually in the present life. To see all illness and disability in this way, however, is to overlook a fundamental part of karma. Ill-health, debility and a weak constitution can also be taken on as a learning experience. The manifestations of karma are subtle and varied.

Karmic Causes of Dis-ease[1]:

- *Soul unrest*
- *Soul intention*
- *The need to develop specific qualities*
- *Past-life repression of pain that refuses to be ignored any longer*
- *Attitudinal karma*
- *Closed-mindedness*
- *Bigotry or lack of empathy for others*
- *Unwillingness to help others*
- *Organic karma*
- *Direct carryover of affliction or disability*
- *Redemptive karma*
- *Non-development of creative potential*
- *Conflict from several past-life personas*
- *Strongly negative past-life self trying to manifest again*
- *Curses or ill-wishing*

How Karma Transfers to a New Physical Body

The physical body is an important part of the karma to be dealt with in a life. It may be one of the trials or challenges of that life. It is clear from regression experiences to the between-life state that most souls about to reincarnate choose the body, and its physical condition, carefully. The body is frequently the 'last stop' for karma as the origin of a physically manifesting karmic condition is rarely physical – unless it is caused by a former life injury. The root cause is most often a thought, emotion, closed-mindedness or spiritual dis-ease manifesting physically. It is as though the karma 'solidifies' in the physical dimension.

The physical body is surrounded by the subtle energy bodies that comprise the aura or etheric body. These energy bodies relate to the emotional mental and spiritual levels of being and they exist after death of the physical body. They vibrate at different rates to the physical body, which is the densest vibration. Psychics see the aura as 'coloured light' radiating out around the body. To a psychic eye, illness or dis-ease shows up as discoloured patches in the aura. Whilst some of these patches may relate to present-life causes, others will be karmic.

At death, the aura or etheric body withdraws with the soul from the physical and moves to another plane, taking with it the imprint from its experiences, whether these be at a physical, emotional, mental or spiritual level. Ingrained thoughts are recorded, fleeting or persistent emotions are registered, and all areas of dis-ease mapped. As the etheric body progresses beyond death, the subtle bodies drop away but the essence of the karmic imprints is carried by the soul as an 'etheric blueprint'. In past-life regression work, people who go into the between-life state often see the etheric blueprint for their next body as a plan which is rather like an architect's drawing. Changes can be made to the blueprint at that stage which will impinge forward into the new life – one of the techniques used in past-life healing. Buddhism and Theosophy postulate a 'permanent mental atom' that carries the karma in a similar way.

When the soul is ready to incarnate again, the etheric blueprint is what manifests the physical body and the new aura – although it may be helped by genetic or in-utero conditions that can create dis-ease or disability. From the moment the soul takes over the new body (and, from regression to the between-life state, it can vary considerably as to timing) the etheric blueprint will begin to build a body that is appropriate to the karma for the present lifetime. If there is karma that will not be dealt with, this is held in suspension. The new body will reflect any fundamental dis-ease in its new aura as well as past-life imbalances or ingrained attitudes. A physical condition that allows the soul to work with karma may manifest from birth or develop at an appropriate time.

So, by way of illustration, if a woman had a past-life history of thinking that life was not sweet enough, bitterly feeling that it was unfair that she should be deprived of whatever it was she wanted, then her spiritual dis-ease would be that she grabbed at love without giving it (the primary cause of selfishness and disaffection). Her new aura would reflect the fact that her etheric blueprint was disturbed over the pancreas – the organ associated with bitterness and a lack of sweetness. She could be born with a propensity to diabetes or low blood sugar levels, or to pancreatic malfunction in later life (see Figure 1).

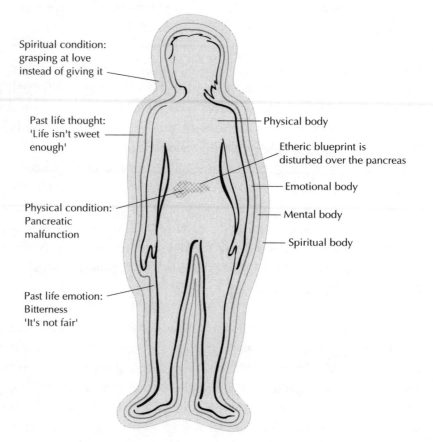

Spiritual condition:
grasping at love
instead of giving it

Past life thought:
'Life isn't sweet
enough'

Physical condition:
Pancreatic
malfunction

Past life emotion:
Bitterness
'It's not fair'

Physical body

Etheric blueprint is
disturbed over the pancreas

Emotional body

Mental body

Spiritual body

Figure 1: How past-life experiences affect the next physical body.

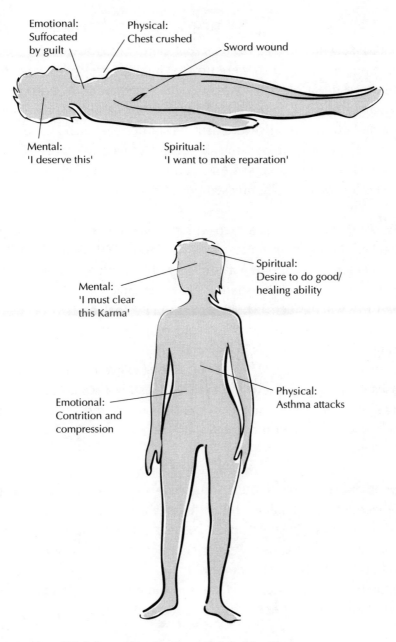

Figure 2: Past-life injury affecting new physical body

One more example may make this even clearer. Edgar Cayce said that those who suffered from asthma had often 'pressed the life' out of someone else and so were now feeling like they were having the life pressed out of them (which could be regarded as both retributive or symbolic karma depending on other factors). I regressed an elderly lady who had severe asthma. In her case, while she herself had not actually pressed the life out of others, that was often the result of the work she was engaged in and, at the end of that life, the breath was literally pressed out of her.

She went back to being a man who received reports from informers, checked them out and then passed them on to the witchfinders. He had become unwittingly embroiled in the work and could find no way to break free. If he tried to protect people, or if he left the job, then the witchfinders would have thought that he had been influenced by the witches and he would have been ducked at best and hung at worst – this was in England where witches were not burned as they were elsewhere in Europe. (Heretics were burnt, and many cases of organic, rather than symbolic, asthma stem back to inhaling smoke on the burning pyres.) If he committed suicide, then, in the beliefs of the time, he would be damned for ever. It was agonizing. He felt suffocated.

Eventually he took a horse and rode off. After pursuit, he was stabbed, causing a fall from the horse which then rolled over, crushing the man's chest. He died gasping his life out and unable to breathe, exactly as she experienced during an asthma attack. The final thought was: 'I deserved this.' We did some healing work in the between-life state and she showed enormous compassion for herself as she had been then.

That work cleared the asthma from her present life. Her etheric blueprint had carried the imprint of the trauma and physical injury; the emotional pain and guilt and the sense of suffocation she had felt; whilst her mental body had carried the belief that she deserved to pay for what she had done. Her spiritual body carried the desire to make reparation for the suffering she had caused to others. Although she had suffered from severe asthma, she had worked as a healer who helped many people during her life. This was her way of making reparation.

Disease as a Way of Balancing out Karma

Diseases are tools which the soul uses in its growth towards a greater state of perfection. Rudolf Steiner in his 'spiritual science' suggests that certain diseases are taken on by a soul as a way of balancing out former actions or tendencies, offering opportunities for developing new strengths. Steiner's belief is supported by reports from hundreds of regressions carried out around the world. Time and again a soul will look for the karmic cause of a dis-ease or condition only to find that it is something they have taken on as a learning situation. Nevertheless, both can be true. The dis-ease may be karmic, and the condition may have been taken on for soul growth. Steiner asserts that 'in karma also lies the curability or incurability of a disease.'[2] In this view, an illness is not only the result of past-life events, it also has the karmic aim of enabling the soul to grow and to fulfil certain objectives.

It is Steiner's contention that pneumonia, for example, would balance out a former life in which the tendency had been towards sexual excess and a desire to live a sensual life. The soul in the present life carries an antipathy towards such behaviour – an antipathy imprinted in the between-life state during a life review. However, Steiner believed that 'forces' imprinted in that state would attract the disease *and* provide the means of overcoming it. In self-healing, the soul would 'lay aside what was a defect in character in a previous incarnation'.[3]

Illness as Spiritual Growth

It is clear from regression work that many souls take on illness as a means of spiritual growth. Rather than being punished for former ills, or for balancing past 'deficits', they identify qualities in themselves such as compassion, tolerance, gratitude and the like which they feel need to be further developed. They may also take on a condition as a way of helping others, either by drawing off collective karma or by offering the other person an opportunity for service that will develop similar qualities within their own self.

A Complex Case

Many cases of chronic illness are a complex mixture of many factors. One of my clients, for instance, suffered from a disease that incorporated, amongst other things, family karma, personal karma including a 'karmic treadmill' and ingrained expectations, redemptive karma, and a desire to grow spiritually.

When she first contacted me she was paralysed from a 'rare, intractable, complex and defeating familial condition, with no known cause, cure or name'. She expressed 'a burning desire to end this misery', not through suicide but by healing. She was the seventh known generation to carry a rare, genetically-transmitted disease. Her matriarchal family interaction was tight. It appeared that the women in the family had together incarnated again and again with this condition manifesting in each generation. She had been taught to view herself as a victim of the family curse from a young age and had the karmic memory of living at least two previous lives with the disease. Her present life had not been easy. Her husband had died just before her daughter was born – a karmic expectation that she held from past lives. It was also clear that in her past incarnations she had not felt comfortable in a physical body.

She used meditation and flower remedies to heal the emotional trauma of past and present lives, and worked to befriend her body. Two years later, her paralysis was gone and she was able to travel to Australia to see a specialist in her condition. She founded an association for fellow sufferers, to give hope and pursue the possibility of a cure; and worked on healing herself so that her own daughter would have a better future. Many shamans say that by healing oneself, it is possible to heal seven generations back and seven forward. It was her sincere desire that this should be so, and that the spiritual insights and qualities she found would be put to work to help other sufferers.[4]

What if the illness cannot be healed?

Sometimes an illness appears to have been healed, then a relapse occurs. Or, the disease proves to be intransigent and ingrained. Looked at from one karmic perspective, if the illness is chronic and cannot be healed, then it may be that the soul needs to have that particular experience for a longer time, the karma cannot be wriggled out of. Whilst some improvement can be brought about by diligent 'work' (karmic balancing), a complete cure may be impossible where a karmic debt or cause is particularly strong. However, Edgar Cayce brought up an interesting point when he asked the question: 'Why does the entity want to be healed?' According to the reading he was doing at the time, the person concerned seemed to want to be healed so that he could satisfy his physical appetites. He was warned that unless there was a sincere change of heart, mind and intent no more help could be given. Spiritual purpose had to be realigned too, and it was up to him whether he accepted, or rejected, the advice.

The man was young, 34, and suffering from multiple sclerosis. In an initial reading he had been told that, whilst his condition was a karmic one, he should not lose hope as help was available if he was willing to accept it. He was exhorted to change his mental outlook, removing all hatred and malice from his consciousness. He was then given a course of treatment to follow. A year later, he contacted Cayce again saying there had been an immediate improvement which was maintained for four months before a serious relapse occurred. With Cayce in trance, it became clear that whilst the man had followed the physical prescription, the spiritual one had been overlooked. He was told '... so long as there is hate, malice, injustice, jealousy, so long as there is anything within at variance with patience, long suffering, brotherly love, kindness, gentleness, there cannot be a healing of the condition of this body.'[5] In other words, he had not got to grips with the lessons that his dis-ease was offering him.

The same scenario occurs in many karmic illnesses. The person wants to be healed so that life will 'return to normal', which entirely misses the point that the dis-ease is making. What was normal is no longer appropriate. Changes have to be made at the spiritual level – and often at the physical as well. Unless the person is willing to do whatever is necessary, a permanent cure cannot be effected because the underlying karmic condition will remain. If the illness is designed to bring to the surface patience and tolerance and it brings up bitterness and intolerance, those feelings will ensure the condition remains. Similarly, if someone then wants to go back to a life of excess and indulgence, and the karmic cause *was* over-indulgence (physical or emotional), the cause will be replayed and a relapse will occur.

Notwithstanding, there is a danger here that the soul, or other people, will be in blame mode. If the soul blames itself, then it does not understand the perfect fairness and dispassionate nature of karma. If it turns to self-pity rather than compassion for itself, a new karmic chain will begin. If other people blame, then they are in judgement mode and no one in incarnation can possibly understand all the reasons why someone takes on an illness. Karma is not a question of punishment or reward, it is a question of finding karmic balance. That this may well entail changing attitudes, beliefs and actions could bring about a karmic cure but there may a deeper, underlying motive. The soul could be practising redemptive karma or offering a lesson to someone else. And, in any case, cure does not equal 'making it better'. The karmic condition may well be cured without the physical ailment improving, if that is the karmic necessity. The soul will only understand the full ramifications when it returns to the spirit world.

And if the illness ends in death?

Western medicine tends to look on death as a failure. A cure has not been effected. But karmically, the opposite can be true. The karma could well have been balanced out by *the experience of the illness*, not by getting rid of it. The cure lies in the qualities developed and through overcoming dis-ease at a spiritual level. As Rudolf Steiner points out, if the illness or condition has been taken on in order to learn or to develop certain qualities, and if the soul has found a point where the physical body and other 'forces' do not disturb it, equilibrium has been reached. There is nothing more to be gained from the illness or condition. The person could recover but the remainder of that life may not then offer any more opportunities for karmic growth. The soul may, in that case, choose death so that it can move onto another life in which the lessons can be developed further. So there could well be karmic reasons why an illness can be cured, or not, and why someone dies at an early age. This is not a punishment, it is a reward.

Short Life Spans

An issue that is often raised is why some people have short life spans. Is this a punishment? Or is it intentional? From regression work both I and other people have carried out in the between-life state, it is clear that souls may have widely different reasons for undertaking a short life. Souls may have had an extremely traumatic death in the last life, or may have committed suicide. They may well then choose to have a 'peaceful interlude', a short life which enables them to gently acclimatize to the idea of being in incarnation again. A soul who committed suicide in the past may choose to live out the time remaining from the 'interrupted life'. Another soul might be on a karmic mission and, once that mission is completed, they may decide then to return to the spirit world.

I had a close friend whose child died just as she was entering her teens. Naturally her mother was distraught, but the child had remained in a coma for a few days prior to her death and she constantly appeared to her mother in dreams. She told her that, now that they had established contact, it was her time to leave the physical world but that she would be with her mother from the spiritual realm. Once the mother had overcome her initial grief, she became a counsellor who worked with parents whose children had died. Psychic from birth, she used her gifts to bring comfort to the parents and to help them come to terms with their loss. Her daughter acted as a 'guide', bringing messages from the children who died and aiding them in their progression on the other side.

Some children may well come to bring their parents a lesson. Michael Newton reports a case where a client had died from a birth defect in a previous life. During the regression, he was asked: 'What was the purpose of your life ending when you were only a few days old?' His reply was that the lesson had been for his parents, not for him and that was why he had elected to come back with them for a short time. Apparently, in another life, those parents had abused a child who eventually died. In their next incarnation, despite being extremely loving parents, they had needed to experience the loss of a child they desperately wanted. In other situations, through caring with great love and compassion for a dying child, parents develop within themselves qualities that they wished to build, or they support a child while he or she goes through an experience they need.

From my experience, it is virtually impossible to identify the reasons why someone has a short lifespan without a karmic reading being done by someone who is able to see further than the present life. Occasionally, regressing a parent to the between-life state may reveal the underlying cause. And, it is clear that a number of children who die 'early' then return to the family once again.

Organic Karma and Chronic Disease

Organic karma reflects injuries or conditions from other lives. Over-indulgence, for instance, could manifest as obesity or liver problems. Too much blood-letting in the past could create anaemia. A previous life back injury could underlie a chronic back problem; tuberculosis could result in present-life lung disease and so on. According to Edgar Cayce sexual excess in one life can lead to epilepsy in the next life, whilst Rudolf Steiner thought that it would result in pneumonia. Epilepsy in the present life may also be created by a misuse of psychic gifts in a previous life or by spiritual initiations which failed. The energy field is disturbed, creating imbalances in the etheric blueprint from which the new body develops. According to the theosophist Annie Besant, epilepsy can also arise from alcoholism in a previous life, the soul being attracted to a family whose genetic code has been damaged by alcoholism so that there is a propensity towards diseases of the nervous system.

Positive organic karma can arise when the soul has worked hard to strengthen an organ such as the heart in a past life. This positive karma can stand the soul in good stead when illness or disability must be overcome.

Organic karma can also arise from soul choices that have caused other people to suffer, and when the soul reincarnates, it has to learn what it feels like to go through that pain or trauma. According to Edgar Cayce, the glands of the body are often utilized in manifesting karma at a physical level. The glands are sensitive to psychic and psychosomatic input and can reflect karmic dis-ease. So, someone suffering from a hormone or brain-chemical imbalance could be put in a position where they were unable to function socially and could well indulge in behaviour which they, in former times, would have condemned.

An example Cayce gives is that of a former-life nun who had been 'stern, cold and intolerant of human weakness'. As a teenager, an endocrine imbalance caused severe menstrual flow. She was unable to have a normal social life, becoming very shy and reclusive. She did not learn how to make relationships. Later, she became a well-known model – put on a pedestal and viewed by other people but lacking contact with them. When she married, it was to a stern, cold, intolerant man. Starved of affection, she became intolerably lonely when her husband was posted overseas during World War II. She moved to a resort town, drinking heavily and indulging in 'loose living'. At first her drinking was to overcome her social inhibitions, but soon she was permanently drunk. Drink made her throw aside all her inhibitions. This former nun would take off all her clothes and go out in public stark naked. In meeting other people's condemnation of her actions, she met herself face to face. In her previous life, she had had a meanness of spirit that condemned everyone who did not live up to her own high standards. Now she learned at first hand what it was to hunger uncontrollably for something, and understood the overwhelming need to deaden the pain of loneliness with whatever was to hand.

Affective Karma

Affective karma builds over several lives. The physical body in the present life is affected by what has gone before at an emotional or mental level. It arises out of an intransigent attitude, ingrained behaviour or an intractable or habitual emotional stance. It often

95

manifests at the physical level: a physical condition being a manifestation of soul dis-ease. So, for example, Edgar Cayce stated that there was a strong link between pride in a previous life and crippling disfigurement in the present life. Attitudes such as believing there would 'never be enough', or that there always has to be more, could precurse an addiction. Arterial or heart problems can develop from 'hard-heartedness' or a former broken heart, or from being too open-hearted. Edgar Cayce asserted that no one could hate his neighbour and not have a liver or stomach disorder, and that jealousy would produce digestive orders or heart conditions. Mental states such as doubt can also affect the next life. Cayce said that doubt in one life almost inevitably led to fear in the next; and from there to dislike, hatred and anger. '... within the inner, psychic world of man there are a throng of weaknesses and imperfections – selfishness, stupidity, envy, malevolence, and greed – that are the source of pain both to himself and to those with whom he lives.'[6] Such weaknesses ultimately affect the health of the incarnating soul's vehicle – the physical body.

Rudolf Steiner believed that ingrained attitudes developed across lifetimes and arose out of an imbalance in the soul. So, for instance, someone who had a tendency towards telling lies would do so because he was not in touch with his inner guidance. A life previous to that would have been 'superficial' and shallow. The person would not know what it was to love or to be devoted to anything, resulting in 'unsteadiness' in character. In the life lived after the one in which lies were told, the person would have, in Steiner's opinion, 'incorrectly formed organs'[7] because something would be out of balance in the soul and that would result in a 'weak organization' in the body. This would not be a punishment for lying, it would arise from the soul having, in the between-life stage, had a revulsion against itself for not telling the truth. According to Steiner, deeds in one life will be transformed at death into a powerful emotion. This emotion imprints on the soul so that the overall quality of the way of being in the previous life is reflected in the present disposition and physical structure.[8]

Illness and Previous Injury

Illness may be a dis-ease of the soul or the imprint of previous trauma. The English psychiatrist Arthur Guirdham found that specific parts of the body were subjected to repeating patterns of injury and it is quite usual during regression work to find that a 'bad back', for example, is the reflection of a previous injury.

One woman, for instance, discovered that she had been paralysed during a life as a sailor. A spar had fallen onto the sailor's back, exactly where her present-life pain was. But another dimension of karmic injury or illness was shown in the remainder of that past-life story. Confined to a chair, he became severely frustrated and angry, lashing out verbally at the dutiful daughter who cared for what she described during the regression as 'a broken hulk'. It was this bitterness which created a karmic imprint – and a karmic enmeshment between the two of them. In the present life, the daughter had returned to her. But she was not so dutiful, rebelling against her mother when she tried to control her. Every time the daughter rebelled, the mother would take to her bed with backache, compelling the daughter to look after her. It was a cycle that was difficult to break. Even after the daughter married and left home, the mother would demand her presence. She found it impossible to let go. In past-life therapy some progress was made as she was taken into the between-life state to look at what she was creating by perpetuating the karmic cycle. But, in the end, she preferred to keep her illusion of control over her daughter rather than change her attitude. This carrying forward of an ingrained attitude is a major factor in chronic karmic dis-ease.

Ill-Wishing

The consequences of ill-wishing in a previous life can be surprisingly strong. They have two ways of manifesting. If the ill-wishing has 'stuck' to the person concerned, then they might manifest an illness or condition which reflects the ill-wishing. Such ill-wishing does not have to be deliberate. Simply thinking: 'I hope he gets what's coming to him,' is enough to set the karma in motion. The ill-wishing may also rebound on the person who had the thought in the first place. In regression, a woman with an ulcerative skin condition was surprised to find that she had, in a former life, voiced the hope that someone would 'rot in hell' for what he had done to her. A few lives down the line, she herself manifested the 'rot'.

Curses are a more serious problem. They carry 'malice aforethought' and a much more powerful karmic charge. Many protracted illnesses and states of disease can arise out of old curses (as can unfortunate life circumstances). If the curse is made by or with the assistance of someone trained in the magical arts, the intention remains 'alive'. No ancient Egyptian would be without an amulet designed to ward off evil spells. In regression, I once had to go back to smash a clay tablet inscribed with a curse which was quite definitely having an effect on my health in my present life. Artefacts may still be around today that express the curse. In the Roman baths at Bath, for instance, hundreds of lead plates have been found with curses inscribed. Some are specific and personal but others were generic.

The karma attached to a curse may be very long-lasting indeed. It may pass through family lines as well as through one particular soul's experience. Both the recipient of the curse and the person who placed the curse may be pulled together life after life as they are tied tightly by invisible bonds. Each may in turn experience physically the result of that curse. Much work may be needed to break the karmic cause.

Phobias

Phobias often have a karmic cause and stem from irrational, overwhelming and exaggerated fear. They have a past-life root directly related to the present-life fear and for this reason can be called karmic. Action in the past is producing a reaction in the present. Drowning can create a terror of water, falling off a high tower induces a fear of heights, a tunnel collapsing brings on claustrophobia, for instance. Such fears are very specific. A woman who drowned in a deep, still pool was terrified of deep, calm water but was quite happy on a fast-flowing river or the heaving sea. Other people have found that death by snakebite leaves a lasting fear of these creatures.

Some phobias can be symbolic. A woman who was terrified of spiders found that, in a previous incarnation, she had had her hand chopped off. When it fell to the floor, it looked rather like a spider. When she incarnated again, spiders reminded her of that old trauma and all the fear transferred itself.

Phobias like these are a deeply-ingrained reaction to the particular stimulus. A woman became terrified whenever she was wrapped in anything tight. If she tried on a dress that had no back opening and became stuck with it over her arms and head, she would scream and become hysterical. If she became entangled in the bedclothes at night, the same reaction would occur. But if someone put their arms around her and held her tight, although she would struggle, she would not scream. In past-life regression, she found that she had had a sack tied over her head and upper body before being hit over the head and thrown into a river to drown. Her phobia was specific to the part during which she was conscious: material over her face, head and arms with darkness and the inability to move being the phobic trigger. The drowning took place when she was unaware of what was happening to her and did not have an immediate karmic consequence. Through past-life therapy, she was able to heal the memory and the phobia faded.

However, past-life therapy brought up an interesting aside. When she was young her mother held her underwater whilst teaching her to swim. This terrified her and she would cling to the side whenever she went swimming with her mother. This went on for years although she was by then a competent swimmer away from her mother. In the regression, the mother was one of the people who threw her into the water.

Phobias can be more complicated than this, having an underlying karmic cause such as suppressed aggression, guilt or antagonism. This suppressed feeling becomes inextricably linked to the phobic trigger and may result in claustrophobia, agoraphobia and the like. This is rather like attitudinal or affective karma. It is the result of the emotional stance taken at the time (no matter how suppressed) and what the person is experiencing in the present life stems from that old attitude. They are, in effect, punishing themselves and need to learn to break the cycle of stimulus–response, action–reaction.

Phobias can also arise from emotions experienced on someone else's behalf. Edgar Cayce gave a reading to a woman who was terrified of wild animals. He said she had watched her previous-life husband being forced to fight wild beasts in the Roman arena. Her fear for him then transferred to her own fear in the present. There are times when fears are not quite phobias, and they occur because they remind the person of a previous event. In regression, a client of mine found, quite incidentally, that her fear of watching other people standing in unprotected high places came from having been blown off a high cliff herself. This had not prevented her from standing in similar places herself in her present life and it was only when she saw someone else doing it that the fear kicked in. In the regression, she found that she had been relieved to die – it had not been an easy life. What bothered her was that someone else's life might be brought to a premature close in a similar way. She carried that fear forward into her new life.

Psychological Dis-ease

Not all karmic disease manifests physically. The dis-ease may occur on an emotional or mental level. Many cases of schizophrenia and mental breakdown have a background of past-life trauma: the soul may have been tortured or endured powerful emotional dramas, for instance. They can also indicate a fundamental conflict and imbalance arising from two very different past-life personalities trying to integrate, or a past-life personality trying to take over the present-life one. But this is not the only way such conditions can arise. A past-life injury can create an etheric block that presents as a chemical imbalance in the present-life brain. Psychic disturbances from the past are also common causes of psychological dis-ease. If someone has failed a psychic or spiritual initiation in a former life, that can manifest as psychological disease in the present. It may take the form of recurrent nightmares or have a more serious manifestation such as epilepsy.

From past-life regressions, it is clear that some temple initiations used imagery and the power of the mind, whilst others used actual objects to test a pupil. Many people have regressed into lives where they faced an initiation to check how well developed their psychic and spiritual powers were. They would be required to face a 'journey', which often entailed meeting, or crossing, a 'pit of snakes'. If the journey was through the mind, the soul had to remember that it was all an illusion. If the journey was a physical one, there were spells and incantations to awaken the power of 'snake charming'. Should the soul waver, the initiation failed and several people have experienced lives where the remainder of their time was lived in fear and psychiatric disturbance. Some of these people have found an echo in their present life – maybe as phobias but also as mental disturbance. The soul may need to go through spiritual initiation again, but in a different way. It may be that the soul has to heal that old scar or to recognize that it was all an illusion.

Depression may also arise from past-life causes – suppressed anger and rage being an emotional cause, as are loss and grief. Overwhelming confusion or loss of hope may also manifest in the present life as an underlying depression but spiritual dissatisfaction can also lie behind this ubiquitous condition. If a soul has lost touch with its spiritual roots or purpose, if it cannot remember why it is in incarnation, or is vaguely aware that 'I should be doing something with my life,' dis-ease will be manifest.

Sexual Dysfunction

Many of the difficulties people experience in their sex lives have their roots in the past. Women who have a fear of sex, often with accompanying anorgasmia, find that they have been raped or forced to have unwelcome sexual congress in a past life. It is hardly surprising that the memory lingers and, even when everything seems on the surface to be willing and loving, the old memory kicks in.

A man who approached me to find the cause of his premature ejaculation went back to a time when he had a passionate affair with a servant girl employed in his house. The affair consisted of hurried fumblings in the linen cupboard and similar locations. He was always enjoining her: 'Hurry, hurry, before my wife finds out,' or 'Quick, before someone comes.' It was hardly surprising that his body still obeyed that command, especially as he set up a similar situation by attempting sex with his first girlfriend whilst his parents were downstairs. The anxiety that they would be discovered by an irate parent brought the in-built pattern to the surface once more.

In this case, the man was repeating an old pattern. In other cases, the soul might have set up the condition of premature ejaculation, or impotence, as 'retributive karma'. They could have felt guilty about sex in the past and the guilt would manifest in the sexual dysfunction. There are, however, more complex cases. Edgar Cayce was consulted by a beautiful woman who had, for eighteen years, been married to a man who was impotent. She was a sensual and affectionate women who craved sexual contact. As she loved her husband, she could not simply leave him. Initially, she had many affairs but found them unsatisfactory. Taking up meditation, she became celibate. Then an old flame turned up again, and passion burned brightly once more. However, this man was married and she

103

did not wish to hurt his wife. Apparently, he had loved the woman from childhood, but she had not known – he was determined to be able to support a wife before he told her. By the time he could, the woman was engaged to someone else. When they met again, the old feelings were there but neither wanted to hurt their partner.

Naturally, this woman was confused by the situation and turned to Edgar Cayce and, most unusually, supplied him with details. Gina Cerminara, who reports the case, says that the past causes of the problem 'inspire a sense of awe, almost, at the singularly appropriate punishment which two erring souls are meeting.'⁹ Apparently, the woman had in a previous life also been married to her present husband. He had gone away to the Crusades but before he went, he put his wife in a chastity belt. The wife deeply resented the lack of trust and 'vowed to get even'. As Cayce put it in the reading: 'Being forced to remain in a state of chastity caused the entity to form detrimental determinations. That this has become a portion of the entity's present experience, then, is only the meeting of self.'¹⁰

In analysing the 'retributive justice', Gina Cerminara says that the man who used mechanical means to impose chastity on his wife was rewarded by impotence. On the surface, the fact that the woman should again endure sexual frustration is, at first sight, difficult to understand. However, Cerminara says that it was her reaction to his unjust action, and her desire for revenge, that created the karmic situation between them in the present life. In the present life, she was utterly desirable and yet her husband was unable to respond – this was his karmic retribution. Had she desired to get even, she could have taunted him with her affairs. However, in the meantime she had grown in spiritual understanding and could not bear to hurt either her husband or this man's wife. In 'meeting herself' in the situation, she found the way to redeem the past karma. With Cayce's Christian background, she was allowing, in his terms, 'vengeance to be taken by karmic law not herself.'

THE KARMA
of Work

Although career choices may seem to be random, or based on family expectation, they may well relate to karma. The karma of work arises from previous employment or vocations, past behaviour, ethical decisions or choices made. Previous lack of integrity, for instance, could manifest as someone who, in this life, has a business partner who commits fraud. A factory owner whose working practices caused many accidents could reincarnate as someone who had a great concern for safe working practices. Positive work karma, on the other hand, creates skills and vocations in the present life. Edgar Cayce frequently gave career guidance based on a previous life. He told someone who had once been in charge of a king's wardrobe in the past, for instance, to find a job connected with fabric and costume as this would use his natural talents.

Technological Karma

The karma of technology stems from having had to make ethical decisions about the use, or misuse, of technology in the past. It can also apply to having fought against the introduction of new technology – especially when this would have been beneficial to humankind. So, for instance, a man in regression went back to being part of an English Luddite group who went around the country smashing up new mill machines which were taking over people's jobs. He was not surprised. He told me that his present-life work involved retraining people who had been made redundant. He taught them computer skills as these were the most likely to be required long term. He had gained his own computer skills after he lost his job as a printer. Whilst being retrained to use the new automated technology, he 'felt like a machine, there was no skill or soul in the work anymore, I wanted to smash it up,' and so he became a teacher of others to help them find their way in this 'alien landscape'.

107

Technological karma can relate to all periods in history but often involves industrial and technological revolutions and their effects on modern life. It can also occur with someone who misused or was abused by technology in the past and now finds it difficult to adapt to modern technology. Someone who, in a past life, was severely injured by machinery may well have an in-built fear and gravitate towards more artistic or soil-based work, for example.

Vocational Karma

In vocational karma, work and skills are carried over from another incarnation. A soul who has been a doctor, for instance, may bring into the present life the urge to heal. If the previous incarnation was more than two or three hundred years ago, then a knowledge of herbal medicine will probably be present and could well lead to an interest in pharmacology or complementary therapies. A former monk or nun could well feel that they still have a vocation, a musician could heed the urge to continue with music.

I did a karmic reading for a doctor who asked me to look at why he had become a doctor despite coming from a family of engineers. 'It was something I had to do,' he wrote. I saw him as having been a doctor in Edinburgh in the nineteenth century. A doctor who used corpses so that he could study the flow of blood around the body – and who faced considerable repercussions in that life when the source of his research was made public. In another life, he had been a barber-surgeon – practising blood-letting. He was connected to a factory where lead was used to make paint and child labour was employed. He tried to deal with the consequences of environmental pollution which had come about, he surmised, through some kind of poison in the water. This made him exceedingly unpopular with the factory owners. Unbeknown to me, in his present work he specializes in diseases of children's blood. He was particularly interested in environmental factors and their effect – especially that of air-borne lead near to major roads. Clearly he had carried his past-life interests forward. He also carried some of the conflict forward. The resistance in England towards his research work on environmental factors was so strong that he had to go to America to find recognition.

Vocational karma is an opportunity to capitalize on past skills and abilities. Edgar Cayce told one man that he had spent many lives working on frescoes for temples, law courts and seats of government. He advised him to take up architecture once he had left art school and to 'combine the modernistic with the Phoenician and Egyptian'. The man did as he was advised and became a leading fresco artist. In another reading, a young woman was advised to give up being a telegraph operator and to take up commercial art as she had been a competent artist in several former lives. It is reported that not only did she become a highly successful commercial artist but she also 'transformed her personality in the process'.[1]

Edgar Cayce also traced how a series of lives can interact to bring someone to the highest expression of their vocational karma. He told a successful New York arranger and composer that he had had four incarnations which were especially relevant to his present-life work. In one, he had been a teacher in New York who had been responsible for introducing music classes to the school curriculum; in the second he had been a German wood carver who made musical instruments; in the third he had been 'jester' to the court of King Nebuchadnezzar, and in the fourth he had been in the temples of Egypt working with music. In his present life, his insistence on perfect tone in instruments arose from the German incarnation. His strongly-developed sense of fun and wit came from the jester incarnation and his musical abilities from the two other lives.

Vocational Frustrations

It is not always possible to follow a vocation. Lack of finance or education may interfere, as can physical characteristics or temperamental unsuitability. It may not be appropriate for the soul to continue with previous work, although there may be a strong urge to do so. It may be time to move on to other things, to develop talents in a different area. But there may be underlying causes which are much less obvious. There are cases in the Cayce files where vocational choices were unable to be fulfilled and the subjects turned to Cayce for guidance as to why. In his view, such 'vocational frustrations' arose out of 'spiritual defects' which needed to be corrected and which would not have been overcome had the person followed their vocation.

In one such example, Cayce read for an extroverted, highly talkative woman who had an aggressive, pushy nature. Her short, squat body combined with difficult family circumstances made it impossible to fulfil her ambition to be an actress so she entered the world of business. Cayce identified her as an entertainer during the American Revolution who had sacrificed personal principles to achieve social status and a luxurious lifestyle. Her ability to communicate freely and her out-going personality had passed into the present life, together with a tendency to talk people into doing what she wanted but Cayce said that, in the other life, she had used her gifts 'without spiritual insight' and, therefore, she had been frustrated in putting her undoubted dramatic talent to use. She was specifically warned to ensure that, in the present life, she did not put her 'expressive gifts' to work without supporting them with spiritual understanding.

The inference was that, if she did, something worse would befall her. As a compensation for her past behaviour, and to bring out the best in herself, she was advised to use her talents in storytelling for children or the disadvantaged. In this way, she would use her gifts unselfishly for the good of others and balance out her karma.

As Edgar Cayce advised: 'Determine your ideal, your inner life goal, and seek to accomplish it.'[2] He also suggested that the most appropriate vocational choice was one which offered the opportunity of being of service to others as this brought about soul growth and collective evolution.

Hobbies and Pastimes

There are occasions when it is not appropriate to continue a past skill at a vocational level, but it can still be expressed as a hobby. Many women have needlework skills that were developed in former lives, but an elderly man was surprised to find that he had an innate talent for tapestry work. In a past life, he had been a woman who supervised the making of tapestries for a large castle. Many other people who work with wood or have similar abilities find that they had been earning a living using the same skills in the past.

Edgar Cayce gives the example of a banker whose past lives gave him considerable abilities in the financial field, which he chose to develop in the present life. He was, however, an avid baseball fan and ran a baseball training club in his spare time. Cayce traced this back to his having been the manager of the state games in Roman times.[3]

Hobbies may become so absorbing that they lead to full-time employment as life develops. Another man Cayce read for was involved with gems as a hobby initially, whilst serving in the navy, and then as a full-time occupation when he retired. When Cayce looked at his past lives, he had been a trader on several occasions and dealt in precious stones. He had supplied stones for priest's vestments and so understood their religious significance; and he appreciated them as objects of great beauty that would appeal to collectors. Cayce told him that despite this, he had never really recognized their true value. In his present incarnation, he was urged to comprehend how the vibrations gems gave off could cure disease and so on. (This was long before crystal healing came back into fashion.) After his reading, the man devoted the remainder of his life to studying the more esoteric properties of gemstones.

EIGHT

THE KARMA OF

Communication

The power of words is very strong. Their impression can be indelible and lasting. A lie can blight a life. Disparaging laughter, cruel words and sarcasm impact as strongly as a physical blow, if not more so. Long after a physical hurt has been forgotten, words echo in the mind. Words of all kinds: inadvertent, deliberate, tactful, tactless, insulting, repressive, encouraging, complementing.

It is both the *how* and the *what* of that which was communicated that can lead to communication karma – positive or negative. Words have been used to stir revolutions, to revile and condemn people, and to gain power over others. They have coerced, bedazzled and persuaded. Words can encourage and cajole, support and empower. Some people might sincerely believe that what they teach is the truth, when really it is a perversion of the truth. People have passed on gossip and scandal, made or ruined other people's reputations. They have told truths and untruths; been open and honest or secretive and devious. Some communication is very personal, other transmissions are universal. All have karmic consequences.

In the New Testament, Jesus says: 'Every idle word that men shall speak, they shall give account therefor in the day of judgement. For by thy words thou shalt be justified, and by thy words thou shalt be condemned'.[1] In other words, when the karmic reckoning falls due it is words just as much as actions that will be taken into account. Jesus also declared: 'It is not that which goeth into the mouth that defileth a man, but that which cometh out of the mouth,'[2] and he specifically links how a man is in his heart with what he says: 'A good man produces good from the store of good within himself; and an evil man from the evil within produces evil. For words that the mouth utters come from the overflowing of the heart.'[3]

The effect of communication karma is usually felt in a new incarnation. It can be the cause of physical ailments such as deafness or speech defects; mental or neural imbalances or blockages leading to dyslexia or perception problems; or situations such as misunderstanding, slander, and so on where boomerang or retributive karma rebounds on the soul. What was said – or thought – by the soul comes back to that soul. If the soul has used positive thought and has spoken constructively, then 'merit karma' may well have accrued. However, communication karma can indicate longstanding difficulty in expressing thoughts, feelings and beliefs which is reflected in the present. Such difficulties may also be part of a repeating inability of the soul to express itself. One man who found it difficult to string together even the most simple of sentences, traced back a long line of incarnations with communication impediments of one kind or another. Eventually, he came to the core. He had revealed a secret and inadvertently brought about another's death. He had vowed never to speak again.

Ideological Karma

Attachment to an idea or religious faith, no matter how worthy, can create ideological karma. Someone may have a sincere belief but because of their strong attachment to that belief, often accompanied by a resultant closed-mindedness, karma is created. As Dr Hiroshi Motoyama has pointed out: 'Karma results from mental attachment to an emotion, no matter how ideal. Attachment to a sustained love of knowledge, truth, or wisdom, for instance, produces long-lasting karma.'[4] He goes on to point out that the adherents to a religion are often more attached 'to their own self-righteousness than to the ongoing process of self-realisation'.

Dr Motoyama feels that scholars and scientists can also fall into the same trap and my experiences would support this. They may be so attached to their own particular theory or way of looking at the world that, even in the face of contradictory evidence, they cling to it. This is because considerable emotion is invested in what appears to be an intellectual matter. The emotions concerned have to do with pride, vanity, egotism and ambition. They are so powerful that they block out reason, and create karmic attachment. The more passion invested in a belief, the stronger the karma it creates, which is why the Tibetans consider closed-mindedness to be one of the major factors in disease.

Imposing beliefs on other people also creates ideological karma. The beliefs may be religious, philosophical or purely secular. The means used to impose them may be tyrannical and dictatorial – enforced coercion – or they may be subtle and persuasive – gentle inducement. But the resulting karma is the same. Former teachers and law-makers or enforcers, may well have ideological karma to deal with as do those who were engaged with religious dogma. One man, Mac, regressed to being a Jesuit priest who forcefully converted a tribe in Africa. In his present life, Mac went back to the country on voluntary service to teach his bricklaying skills as a way of making reparation. Then, when he developed lung and throat cancer, he believed that it was his way of working off that old communication karma.

However, in his present life, Mac had also counselled many people and helped them towards spiritual insights, so he believed that, once the present life was over, his karma would be balanced out. Indeed, he was convinced that, having lived in a squat for many years, being able to die in a pleasant nursing home with caring staff to help his death was his 'good karma'.

The power that a belief from a former life can hold over a mind was graphically illustrated by Mac as he was dying. I sat with Mac as he lay in a coma. Although he had chosen not to have treatment, saying that it was his time to pass on, he seemed to be fighting hard to stay alive. Earlier, he had pulled out his drip and run amok. He had clearly been very frightened indeed and his nurses called me and another of his friends to help him. By the time we got there, he had been heavily sedated and given morphine. He could not speak but responded, when I asked him to breathe out his fear, by letting out a long, shuddering breath so I knew he could hear me. I tried to talk him through releasing from his body, reading the *phowa* prayer from Tibetan Book of the Dead as he had requested (see chapter Eleven). He would stop breathing for long periods, and then shiver and begin again.

Realizing that he was in spiritual trouble, I entered into his world with him. He was surrounded by a ring of hellfire. The vivid beliefs about hell he had held as that Jesuit priest in the former life had returned to taunt him. Taking his hand, I said: 'Well, Mac, you always wanted to try fire-walking, how about we give it a go?' We walked together towards the flames, which parted, forming a corridor of fire that burnt off his karma. He died peacefully and shot up a tunnel of light to the spiritual realms.

It is not only at death that such experiences occur. Irrational beliefs, fears and the like are almost always based on previous life experiences. The words that people use in regression often prove to be a key to a strong belief or thought that has been carried over, unrecognized, from another life. That credo or thought will have played a powerful part in creating the present reality and, as such, forms part of communication karma.

Karma of Hypocrisy

Saying one thing, or doing things a certain way, and yet believing something different; lying most sincerely; or pretending to be something you are not, gives rise to the karma of hypocrisy. Hypocrisy arises from a lack of spiritual conviction and inner truth, or a betrayal of truth. A life then arises when that inner foundation has to be regained.

There are people who will do anything for a quiet life. They go along with what is suggested, they agree when something is said that offends their deepest sensibilities, they avoid conflict at all costs. Such people are, on the deepest level, hypocrites, and will reap the karma of hypocrisy. The karma may return in situations where they are put on the spot, where they have to speak their truth. They may speak their truth, and yet not be believed. They may speak their truth and be reviled for it. Or they may find themselves faced with someone who is a hypocrite and cannot be relied upon. Situations such as these ultimately create a congruence between the outer show and the inner feelings as the soul can no longer bear the tensions engendered when the two conflict.

Karma of Mockery

Mocking other people's afflictions, thoughts, beliefs or actions gives rise to the karma of mockery. It is based on not valuing the pathway that another person travels. One such example is when someone else is verbally debased in some way. A person may judge the circumstances of someone else and mock them through words. The person who mocked in a past life often finds him- or herself living out in the present life the circumstances s/he so despised back in that other life.

Edgar Cayce told a crippled polio victim that his illness was the karma that accrued from having been in the audience in Rome when the Christians were thrown to the lions. The crowd had mocked and jeered and he had been carried along with it. It took almost two thousand years for the karma to return.

Condemnation and Criticism

Those who previously condemned or criticized others may have to meet within themselves the very things they found fault with in the past. As Edgar Cayce put it: 'As you have criticized, know that you yourself must be criticized.'[5] So, for example, someone who was intolerant of others and who condemned 'weakness' could well find themselves undergoing an incarnation where they become a drug addict so that they would know what it is to have to confront an apparent weakness – and to be condemned for it by others. A person who criticized another for ignorance could well then find that the next incarnation involved being an uneducated person who appeared, to those who had received a superior education, to be ignorant but who, in fact, had innate wisdom.

Edgar Cayce gave a reading for a young man who suffered from a dreadful sense of inadequacy which held him back in his career as a lieutenant in the army. The inadequacy was brought about by intense self-criticism. Nothing he did was good enough. Cayce saw him as a literary critic in a previous life. His reviews were caustic and pitiless, with the result that he engendered considerable self-doubt in the writers. Now, in the present life, the pendulum had swung and he himself had to experience self-doubt.[6]

Not everyone who suffers from self-doubt will have made a career out of criticism in their former lives, of course. But many will have criticized others, inadvertently or through mere social chit-chat. Criticism, like mockery, arises out of judging others. It seems to be a condition endemic to the human soul. People talk about other people, criticize their work, their appearance, their friends. They may criticize themselves just as much as others, setting impossible standards to meet. Everyone comments on life and some of it may seem innocuous. However, as Edgar Cayce pointed out on many occasions, there is a heavy karmic price to pay. What is criticized in others – even when it has not been voiced to that person – will be experienced in the future. Motive and intention may mitigate this to some extent. Not everyone will be like the literary critic mentioned above. His karmic crime was to be merciless and so bring about deep self-doubt in others. There was no constructive criticism in his work, he simply tore the work to shreds. But even those who engage in constructive criticism tread a very fine line between helping others and eroding creativity and self-worth.

Coercion and Persuasion

Words have been used for thousands of years to influence how people think. The karma will be different if considerable psychological force is applied, or subtle persuasion. Motive and intent can also be a factor in the karma that arises. If someone sincerely believes that what they are saying will help someone else, no matter how misguided that may be, then there is a different kind of karmic effect from someone who cynically persuades someone else round to their point of view for their own advantage. The former may well have to live out a life where the soul gently finds out how misguided it has been, but the latter is more likely to meet the karmic repercussions head on.

NINE

THE KARMA OF
Relationships

The threads of a relationship can be usually traced back through many lives. Few important relationships begin in the present life and even fewer are the result of chance. Attitudes, actions and inter-actions weave a tapestry of which only a small part can be glimpsed in any one lifetime. Relationship karma has many aspects. It can operate in families, love affairs, friendships and business relation-ships. Souls have a wide variety of reasons for reincarnating together, not all of them based on love.

Reasons For Incarnating Together:
- *Spiritual bonds*
- *Previous relationship carried over*
- *Soul mate connection*
- *Unfinished business*
- *Habit, inertia*
- *Dependence and symbiosis*
- *Lessons to be learned*
- *Attitudes to be transformed*
- *Debt or duty*
- *Attachment to mutual unhappiness or happiness*
- *Vows or promises*
- *Love or hatred*
- *The desire for revenge*

Certain aspects of relationship may be purely personal; the soul meets its in-built expectations and the attitudes that it holds regard-ing love through interaction with other people. Other aspects of rela-tionship are personal to the two, or more, people concerned. They have karma from previous lives together. However, some people get together to work on karmic issues that have nothing to do with the other person in a personal sense, they simply share the same issues.

Expectations Around Love:
- *Love is all there is*
- *Love has to be perfect*
- *Love hurts*
- *If it isn't hurting, it isn't love*
- *I don't need love*
- *There will never be enough love*
- *I don't deserve love*
- *Sexual love is sinful*

Sometimes a bond of true love unites a couple down through the ages, but this is not always so. Hatred can be the cause of powerful attachments, and resentment binds people together. Some people will not let go of someone they 'love', and have to come back with that person until they can do so. The lesson can be painful, especially when the other person does not recognize the 'love' and rejects the supposed soul mate. Some couples find themselves living the consequence of ancient infidelities. Retribution can be part of relationship karma, as can recompense, reparation and enmeshment.

Physical attraction can be particularly strong where couples have known each other in the past, but it is not always appropriate to continue the relationship. It may be that the lessons the souls have come back to work on would be better learned alone. It could be that the intensity of karma makes it inadvisable for the couple to confront it until they have worked on the issues separately. It is possible that the couple do not yet have the spiritual strengths required to resolve the karma or that their purposes in incarnating are incompatible. In such cases, it could be advisable for the couples to pursue other relationships no matter how strong the pull of physical attraction.

In his readings, Edgar Cayce always emphasized that karma was not a matter of debt between couples – although I have found many cases where the people concerned did feel that they had a karmic debt, subtle or otherwise, which they wanted to repay. According to Cayce, the issue was one of personal soul development: 'It is merely Self being met ... not karmic debt between but a karmic debt of Self that may be worked out between the associations that exist in the present.'¹ So, if someone complained that their partner was unloving, it was not that the partner should change but that the person asking for a reading should take that opportunity to redress what Cayce called 'imperfect attitudes'. They themselves would be well advised to seek to become more loving as this would overcome a previous inability to love. Equally, if they found it impossible to love someone, then they should work on being more accepting and tolerant so that they could develop unconditional love.

Karmic Relationship Themes

Positive Service: can occur in families or work situations. One person takes on caring for another or performs a task specifically to help the soul growth of the other – may also occur as inappropriate service if the parties become 'stuck' in the scenario. May also include:

> **Unconditional Love:** an opportunity to love 'warts and all', accepting the other person's right to be as they innately are without forcing change and yet at the same time learning not to be 'trampled on'.

Freedom/Commitment Dilemmas: 'can't live with, can't live without' theme played out over many lifetimes. Present lesson may be to let go, or to definitely commit.

Parent/Child: appropriate or inappropriate acting out of these roles regardless of the actual relationship. For example, the wife who calls her husband 'Daddy', the child who has to parent his or her parent. The roles may stem from a previous interaction.

Victim/Martyr/Rescuer/Persecutor/Scapegoat: codependent and abusive relationships revolve around this pattern: one person is treated as superior or inferior to the other or is identified as 'the cause of the problem'. Can also include:

Enmeshment/Dependence and Collusion: addictive, 'helpless', 'helping' or 'enabling' scenarios keep one person weaker than the other. May reflect past-life symbiosis. An opportunity to practise unconditional love and mutual support, interdependence instead of dependence.

Enabler/Enabled: often found in so-called soul mate relationships, one person holds the power and has a vested interest in keeping the other person helpless.

Betrayer/Betrayed: may arise between adults or parent and child if support is suddenly withdrawn.

Seducer/Seduced: not always sexual, can occur at an emotional or intellectual level.

Dominance and Submission: power and control issues, replay of old 'master/slave' roles.[2]

Sequels to the Past

Edgar Cayce frequently stated that no major human relationship is the result of chance; an opinion with which all karmic counsellors would no doubt agree. From a close study of his many thousands of readings, Gina Cerminara concluded that 'no marriage is a start on a clean slate. It is an episode in a serial story begun long ago.'[3] That does not mean, however, that the parties would necessarily have been together before, it was the issues involved that were the serial story. I do see in my own work couples and members of families who are starting out together for the first time. It is as though working through the issues 'at one remove' as it were, they can be more objective than if they have been over the same old ground together time after time.

For Cerminara, based on the evidence Cayce gave, all relationships are 'sequels to the past' – although her view takes no account of 'karma in the making'. Virtually all the people Cayce read for appear to have been connected within soul groups and some had been in close relationship with each other before. Many incarnated together to continue karmic tasks, to close unfinished business or deal with karma. For quite a number of the people Cayce read for, marriage was a 'repeat performance'. He said that they had had the same partners before. However, there were a number of people whom Cayce warned not to repeat the karmic relationship, and he told others that there were karmic influences that made it unwise to enter into marriage. He affirmed the presence of free will and new choices rather than repeating an old pattern.

Soul Mates

Soul mates are both a powerful karmic fact, and one of the biggest illusions of all time. The origins of the idea of a soul mate are expressed in Plato's description of 'original beings' who had two heads, four arms and legs. These original beings angered the gods with their arrogance, and were split in half. Plato says that ever the two halves will seek each other and that, should they find their 'other half', then there is a danger that one will be subsumed by the other as they lose all interest in anything else. Another difficulty expressed by Plato is that, of the original beings, one third were female, one third male and the remaining third were hermaphrodites. So, if Plato is to be believed, the 'other half' may well be of the same sex and not everyone looks for their soul mate within their own sex – and, in any case, it is clear from regression work that souls can change their gender in different lives, although Plato does not mention this.

Most people believe that they have only one soul mate; someone who will make them feel complete and totally at one. But, in my long experience in looking at karmic relationships, this is rare. Yes, there are couples who go through life after life together. But this may become an unproductive and sterile relationship in terms of karmic learning and, eventually, they have to part.

There are many other people who have several soul mates, sometimes within one lifetime. Often these 'soul mates' are part of a 'soul group' who have travelled together through aeons of time. They may not, on the surface, always appear to be the idyllic soul mate that so many people dream of. It can be quite a surprise for someone who appears to be their most hated enemy, abuser and the like, to actually be a member of their soul group who is helping them to learn a difficult lesson.[4]

Karmic Mutation

Not all relationships improve as they mature. In some the interaction changes subtly and yet the underlying dynamics are the same. So, for instance, a relationship which was violent and abusive in its early manifestations may appear on the surface to be much more kind. And yet, below the surface, cruelty may still be present only this time it will manifest on a more psychological level. Sarcasm, endless put-downs, indifference, self-centredness, infidelity, and the like are all mutations of the previous abuse. The couple may be drawn together by hate and a desire for revenge, or they may truly believe that this is 'love'. Until the karma is neutralized, and the underlying attitude changes, they will be drawn back together time and again. The mutations may be many and varied, but the challenge will remain the same.

> **Soul Groups**
> *A collection of souls who belong together in some way, often having travelled as family or friends for many lifetimes. Not all members of a soul group will be in incarnation at the same time, but many do share lifetimes together taking major or minor roles in the soul dramas.*

However, this does not mean to say that all marriages are between people who have had exactly the same relationship in other lives. In my experience, it may be possible that the parties were married before, but it is equally likely – confirmed over and over again by regression work – that the relationship could have been, amongst many possibilities, as parent and child, siblings, friends and acquaintances, bitter enemies, employer and employee, or master and slave. What is clear, however, is that the issues being worked on are rarely new. They may not have arisen between the parties now in the relationship. It is perfectly possible to share a life with some-one one has never met before, but with whom one has certain karmic issues in common. It is sometimes easier to work on these things at a more objective distance, and the incarnation may well be a preparation for working with the person with whom the karma arose in a future incarnation. Even if the relationship is a sequel to the past, it may be that the partners are trying out a different way of doing things, learning new responses, maybe even changing roles or gender. They could well be exploring interdependence after life-times of dependence or extreme independence. Many karmic issues are expressed in relationship.

Why Some People Never Find Their True Mate

To make life bearable, to avoid loneliness, to provide children, are all 'reasons' given by my clients who ask how they can find their soul mate. Such reasons are inherently selfish, they seek to make the self happy, rather than the other person and that, as Tibetan Buddhism tells us, is not a good basis for a relationship.

What many people are looking for in a partner is someone to make them feel complete, to fill in the gaps, as it were. The doctrine of karma, however, says that they should seek to develop the missing qualities within their own self. So, if they are looking for love, they should practise love at every opportunity – which does not mean becoming promiscuous but rather showing love whenever and where possible, even in the smallest of ways.

Lack of a partner is so often regarded as being a negative condition when it can be a positive one. The single state may have been part of the soul plan for the present incarnation. The soul may be learning the difference between being alone and being lonely. Being alone can bring strength and independence, an ability to be happy in one's own company. It can offer the opportunity for spiritual insights gained through meditation, and the possibility of knowing one's inner self more intimately. Being lonely often brings dependence and barriers. The person shuts off from spiritual comfort or insight and is constantly looking 'out there' for answers.

Souls usually encounter what they expect. So if, at a deep level, the soul feels unlovable, unworthy, inadequate or inferior, *for whatever reason*, this is what will be attracted. One of the most powerful ways to find a true mate can be to learn to love oneself – not in a selfish, self-centred way but in a way which appreciates who and what you are in the fullness of your whole being.

Setting too high standards can be one of the pitfalls in finding a mate. If the previous experience was of 'perfection', then anything else tends to disappoint. If it wasn't, then the soul might have decided it has to be. Many people go into relationship expecting – or demanding – that everything should be instantly right. If it was, there would be nothing to work on! On the other hand, if the soul has always settled for something less, and therefore been disappointed in love, then that expectation will probably manifest once more.

Previous decisions and vows can profoundly affect the ability to attract a mate. If a soul has taken a vow of celibacy in another life, unless this was rescinded there remains a certain 'untouchable air' about that person. They may make subtle movements of distaste and rejection which are perceived subliminally by a potential partner, who backs off. Disappointment or hurt in love, the decision that: 'I'll never risk that again,' can have much the same effect. It is as though the aura freezes. Consciously, the person wants to receive love, but subconsciously, a little voice is saying: 'Remember that decision you made, well it was good sense, you'll only get hurt again.' Once the soul recognizes that voice and, where possible, finds out where it is coming from, then a new attitude is possible.

Pacts and Promises

The pacts and promises made in another life, or in the between-life state, can strongly affect the present. They may involve another person or be personal. If a soul promised to always be there for someone or to 'always look after you', it can create relationship karma. The vow holds the two souls together beyond death.

For example, a woman found her partner at the age of 38. She knew from the moment she saw him that they were 'meant to be together', although their path to a committed relationship was not easy. Before that commitment, she had always been held back from relationship by caring for her alcoholic sister and acting as support to her large family. Now, the woman wanted to have a child but worried about her sister as she 'wanted to be there for her'. In regression, she went back to a life in which she had promised her sickly sister that she would indeed always be there for her. She hadn't envisaged the promise lasting several lifetimes. She reframed her vow 'for one life only' and asked that her sister be helped to make her own spiritual progress. Almost immediately, her sister went into treatment, which proved successful, and my client found that she was pregnant.

Declarations that: 'I'll never have another child/relationship/etc,' or 'I will always love/hate you,' can have a powerful effect through many lives. It can pull couples, or parents and children, into relationship time after time until a way is found to heal the interaction that led to the decision. Even decisions to 'always love you' can be karmically blocking. It may be more appropriate for spiritual growth to let go.

Equally powerful can be the promise to mother a specific soul, to provide them with a physical body in which to incarnate. Such promises are, usually, made in the between-life state and are, of course, forgotten when the 'mother' incarnates. The other soul, however, waits for an opportune moment to incarnate. This can lead to complications if the first soul takes a different life path to the one envisaged.

I had a client who was Chinese and had lived in China for the first 40 years of her life. She had, through a series of apparent 'accidents', become a highly successful business woman. As a teenager, she had been very much in love and had married against her family's wishes. Her husband died soon afterwards, under rather mysterious circumstances. She was four months pregnant and she was left destitute. Her family took her back, on condition that she aborted the baby. Although she would very much have liked to have that child, in her situation she could see no other choice. She then went to work in the family business. She had several affairs, each of which ended in pregnancy and abortion by her choice. (China is a country that uses abortion as contraception and this is not unusual.) She began to travel abroad with her work and started using western contraception, but it failed time after time.

By the time she came to see me, having moved permanently to England, she had lost count of the abortions she had had. When we talked about it, she said that the only child she had wanted was the first one, and yet each time she aborted another potential child, she felt tremendous grief. 'It is as though I am supposed to have that child, no matter what,' she said, 'and yet I know I do not want to bring up a child on my own and I have not found a man I would want to be my child's father. And, in any case, I'm getting too old for pregnancy.'

I took her back to scan her former lives to see if there was a reason for the situation but she could not see anything. I guided her into the between-life state to seek the reason there. She quickly found a soul who was waiting to incarnate through her. She had promised this soul that she would be her mother and the soul was still there, waiting. I suggested she should ask the soul why the promise had been made. The soul said that the woman had been her mother once before, but had died in childbirth. The mother had stayed close to her child to 'watch over her'. When they met up in the between life immediately after the soul's death, they had had a very emotional reunion and the promise had been made there and then. Before incarnating, many years later in earth time, the promise had not been discussed again.

The woman told the soul how her circumstances had changed and how she did not feel able to be a mother. The soul told her that she should stick to her promise. A long dialogue then ensued. The woman kept begging the soul to release her, the soul was angry and felt rejected. I had to step in and suggest to the soul that she should talk to her guides. (I felt that as she had been hanging around the earth plane trying to incarnate at every possible opportunity, she had made little progress since her last life and was 'stuck in a groove'.) Reluctantly she did so, and came back to say that she would go with them. But, she was adamant that she and the woman had unfinished business that would have to be dealt with at some future time. She was not, at that stage, able to offer any forgiveness.

Had she been able to, the women would have renegotiated that promise during the therapy session, but it was not to be. I suggested to her that she should spend five or ten minutes each evening, sending love and forgiveness to the soul and holding compassion for her in her heart. In this way, the situation between them would have been subtly altered by the time she left incarnation. As it was, after a few months the soul appeared to her in a dream and told her that she was ready to let the promise go. Had she not done so, the karmic enmeshment would have continued into the next life.

Karmic Enmeshment

If relationship karma is unfulfilled or unresolved in one life, if someone for whom a soul is responsible (as in parent and child) is not looked after, if someone who seeks their freedom is held onto, if someone else is blamed for the soul's own limitations or inability to move forward, if old promises remain, then karmic enmeshment comes into play.

> **Karmic Enmeshment**
> *A situation where two souls are strongly intertwined due to karmic connections. The souls will incarnate together again and again in an effort to clear the situation.*

To hold others culpable for the limitations a soul puts on itself is to invite karmic enmeshment, and creates a situation where the souls are drawn back time and again as one struggles to become free from the other, while one person feeds off the other. Symbiotic relationships and situations where one person owns the other body and soul – as in master/slave and some marriages – also create the same kind of enmeshment. The lesson is to let go, even of what is passing for love (unconditional love does not hold on). One soul may have to learn to stop blaming the other. If one soul has failed to take appropriate responsibility for another – as in a situation where a child is abandoned, for instance – then releasing the enmeshment may first involve giving appropriate parenting or care, possibly to the extent of caring for someone for an entire life if they are ill or disabled, and then setting the soul free to go on its own journey.

Letting go is an enormous karmic challenge. People do tend to hang on to what passes for love; to the way they feel things should be; to hopes, dreams and illusions. Letting go sets everyone free to take their own path. If it really is true love, if things really should be that way, then it will happen. But if it is not, then the soul is freed by letting go, stepping out of the karma, and moving on.

TEN

KARMIC

Consequences

We have seen how the many and varied forms of karma create new situations and the consequences that can arise from former actions on present lives. Modern esoteric teachers and the ancient sages had a great deal to say about how karma would affect the afterlife in which the soul would find itself after death, and the body that would be developed for the next incarnation.

Modern Esoteric Teachings

How the forces of karma transform themselves into a new body was a question which occupied many twentieth-century metaphysicians. Rudolf Steiner believed that if a man had been controlled by his passions, or emotions, then he would, in the next incarnation, find some obstacle in his own body which he would have to overcome. This would in no way be a punishment, it would be self-created as part of the soul's evolution. In compensating for that, he would balance out his karma. When Steiner examined the after-death process he explained that:

> ... *very special forces indeed are taken into the*
> *human individuality in the time between death*
> *and a new birth ... in the kamaloca [afterlife] the*
> *events of a person's last life, his good and bad*
> *deeds, his moral qualities, and so on, come before*
> *his soul, and through contemplating his own life*
> *in this way he acquires the inclination to bring*
> *about the remedy and compensation for all that*
> *is imperfect in him, and which has manifested*
> *as wrong action. He is moved to acquire those*
> *qualities which will bring him nearer to*
> *perfection in various directions. He forms*

137

*intentions and tendencies during the time up to
a new birth, and goes into existence again with
these intentions. Further, he himself works upon
the new body which he acquires for his new life,
and he builds it in conformity with the forces
he has brought from previous earthly lives ...
From this it may be seen that this new body
will be weak or strong in accordance with the
individual's capacity to build weak or strong
forces into it.*[1]

Steiner believed that a 'certain sequence of events' was set in motion in the karmaloca or between-life state. Following death, a life review would take place in which the person not only saw but felt each and every part of the last life very intensely, especially the emotions. Steiner postulated that this occurred because, in life, the brain and mental processes had filtered the emotions. Now, without that filter, those emotions would be much more powerful during the reliving. So, when the soul re-experienced the anger, fear or aversion, envy and so on which underlay his actions, he would do so vividly and would react by saying: 'I must perfect myself so that I no longer come under the domination of my emotions.' That decision would be attached to his soul and would be imprinted as a force on the body that was created for the next birth. In the new incarnation, the soul would not allow itself to be subjected to those emotions, and a new way of responding to life would have to be created. In this way the soul could compensate for previous actions.

One of the illustrations that Steiner gives is that of someone whose sense of self is very weak. Consequently the person is dependent and passive. Due to this lack of sense of self, the person performed certain actions in a former life. After death, he would first look at the actions which stemmed from his weak 'I'. He would then feel that he must develop forces which would strengthen his sense of self or 'I-ness'. He would also feel that he had to develop a body that would show him the consequences of his 'weak personality'.

In the next incarnation, according to Steiner, he would 'not fully enter into consciousness'. By acting according to subconscious forces, he would meet opposition. In these circumstances, he would have to do all he could to strongly exert his 'I-ness'. Steiner suggests that a person like this would be exposed to a cholera epidemic. Whilst it seems difficult to comprehend that cholera would force someone to assert their I-ness, this is nevertheless what Steiner insists will result. He says that then, in the next incarnation, the soul and the different subtle bodies will work much more closely together.

Giving the example of what happens to someone whose sense of 'I-ness' is overly strong, Steiner says that he will seek an opportunity in the next incarnation to have no limit for his sense of self and so 'he will be led to the unfathomable and to absurdity. These opportunities come to him when karma brings him malaria.'[2] In overcoming this, self-healing will be developed and he will be set on the 'upward path of evolution'.

Most people who explore the between-life state find a broad spectrum of agreement on the stages of choosing the next incarnation, assuming that the soul is aware enough to make a choice – some souls simply bounce back, drawn by ungratified desires. There is a review of all that has been achieved so far, usually in the company of guides and helpers; an identification of certain themes or specific qualities to be incorporated into the new life; and a discussion with others members of the soul group who will incarnate at the same time. The possibilities for a new family are then explored.

Sometimes there will be one option but at other times there will be several, all of which have to be weighed up to see which is most appropriate. This process is universal and is reflected in the most ancient of scriptures although choice is less of a factor here. This may well reflect the soul's evolution and assumption of more responsibility as it matures.

What the Ancients Had to Say

In the Hindu *Institutes of Vishnu*, the hells to which sinners pass after death are graphically described, as is the journey through insect, bird or animal incarnations and finally back to human. As animals and the like, there may well be a symbolism between the 'crime' and the result – a stealer of meat becomes a vulture, for instance.

> *Criminals in the highest degree enter the bodies*
> *of all plants successively.*
> *Mortal sinners enter the bodies of worms*
> *or insects*
> *Minor offenders enter the bodies of birds ...*
> *One who has stolen grain, becomes a rat*
> *One who has stolen water, becomes a water fowl*
> *One who has stolen honey becomes a gad-fly*
> *One who has stolen clarified butter, becomes*
> *an ichneumon*
> *One who has stolen meat, becomes a vulture*
> *One who has stolen oil, becomes a cockroach.*
> *One who has stolen perfumes, becomes a*
> *musk-rat ...*

But even when they reach human incarnation again, they have marks which identify their 'sin':

> *A drinker of spirits, black teeth*
> *A malignant informer, stinking breath*
> *A stealer of food, dyspepsia*
> *A stealer of words, dumbness*
> *A poisoner, a stammering tongue*
> *One who eats dainties alone, shall have*
> *rheumatics.*
> *A breaker of convention, a bald head …*
> *Thus, according to their particular acts are men*
> *born, marked by evil signs, sick, blind, hump-*
> *backed, halting, one-eyed.*[3]

According to Vishnu, it takes many lives of penance to overcome such karmic consequences.

Plato had a somewhat kinder view of the afterlife, although there is still a strong concept of due punishment whilst the soul remains in *Hades*, the Greek underworld. The possibility, however, remains open for the soul to find forgiveness and move on to rebirth. In *Phaedo*,[4] Plato has Socrates vividly describe the different realms found within *Hades*. After the ubiquitous Judgement, those who are judged to have lived a 'neutral life' are sent to the Acheron where they undergo purification and 'are both absolved by punishment for any sins that they have committed, and rewarded for their good deeds, according to each man's deserts.' But 'those who on account of the greatness of their sins are judged to be incurable, as from having committed many gross acts of sacrilege or many wicked and lawless murders … these are hurled by their appropriate destiny into Tartarus, from whence they emerge no more.'[5] If a soul has been judged guilty of a sin which, though great, is redeemable, then they too are cast into Tartarus but only remain for a year until the underground river washes them out again. So, if a soul has, in a fit of passion, offered violence to a parent but spent the rest of their life in penitence, even if they committed manslaughter, they have the opportunity of forgiveness. To find this, they must track down the person they killed or misused whilst they are being carried along by the river. If forgiveness is given, then they are freed from Tartarus. If not, the river takes them back again and a yearly cycle commences from which release is not possible until forgiveness is gained.

The Sixth Book of the *Pistis Sophia*, a gnostic Christian text believed to be as old, if not older than the gospels, gives in great detail the words of Jesus concerning the chastisements of the soul after death. The soul of the slanderer, for instance, is led into:

> ... the chaos before Yaldabaoth and his forty-and-
> nine demons, and every one of his demons fall
> upon it another eleven months and twenty-and-
> one days, scourging it with their fiery whips.
> Thereafter they lead it into fire-rivers and boiling
> fire-seas, to take vengeance on it therein ... they
> carry it to the Virgin of light ... that she may
> judge it ... [she hands it to her receivers who] lead
> it to a water which is below the sphere; and it
> becometh a seething fire and eateth into it until
> it purifies it utterly ... And then [after receiving
> the cup of forgetfulness] they deliver it unto a
> body which will spend its time being afflicted.[6]

If the soul belongs to a murderer or a blasphemer rather than a slanderer, then it is 'destroyed and dissolved utterly' after many chastisements. An arrogant soul ends up in a 'lame and deformed body, so that all despise it persistently'. Future prospects are not much better for a righteous man who has 'done good persistently' but omitted to be initiated. Whilst he will be greeted in the afterlife with 'joy and exultation' when it is time to incarnate again, the poor soul will be given, in addition to the cup of forgetfulness, a cup filled with 'thoughts and wisdom and soberness' which will cause it to 'whip its heart persistently to question about the mysteries of the Light until it find them'. However, the *Pistis Sophia* holds out the hope that any man, no matter how great the sin committed, can neutralize the karma through being initiated into the mysteries. After this, no rebirth will be necessary.

Karma-in-the-Making

An important factor in karmic consequences is that the soul is building *at each moment* the foundations for the future. Each act, thought, word and intention will have consequences in the future. A 'positive', constructive and magnanimous approach to life can balance out previous 'deficits'. So, karma can be changed. But it should be borne in mind that karma is ultimately about balance. Nature abhors a vacuum, and so does karma. It is no use simply eliminating one thing, a positive 'reaction' must also be cultivated. In some spiritual systems, emotion is something to be 'overcome' but it is more harmonious to be a person who stands within their emotions, experiencing them but not overwhelmed by them. Recognizing emotional stimuli and mental triggers aid in getting off the karmic treadmill but new pathways need to be initiated. Letting go of attachment needs the balance of dispassionate non-attachment, as otherwise repression sets in. In-built attitudes and prejudices can be overcome, and beneficial attitudes developed. Inappropriate acts can cease, and actions can be taken that are long overdue. A new pattern of thinking can be created, and spiritual practices incorporated into life. Avoiding excess in any direction is wise, whether it be towards the spiritual or the material. In this way, meritorious karma will be cultivated and the soul will move closer to its goal of spiritual evolution.

ELEVEN

KARMIC
Teachings

Karma has been a part of religion for at least 5000 years, and probably much longer. As there was mass migration of peoples around the ancient world, spiritual ideas spread out in waves and there is a surprising congruence of beliefs about the afterlife and the reward or retribution which will follow acts on earth.

For many people a knowledge of karma conditions their life and shapes their culture. Nowadays, with Buddhism becoming one of the fastest-growing beliefs in the west, more and more people are embracing the idea. But it may surprise many people to recognize that religions such as Judaism and Christianity also have a concept of karma – although it has never been known by that name – and that they too follow the way of karma.

Karma in the East

In eastern religions karma is divine justice and it is what drives the wheel of rebirth. The word *karma* translates as 'action' and describes an on-going process of cause and effect. Karma is an integral part of the teachings of Hinduism and Buddhism, as it is in Jainism. In Jainism, karma is viewed slightly differently, however. It is seen not just as a process but as a substance, invisible and subtle, but nevertheless having solid, material form. This substance, in the form of minuscule particles, interpenetrates soul or living substance causing bondage to the cycle of rebirth. All these religions agree, however, that there is a chain of cause and effect at work.

In the Hindu *Bhagavad-Gita* the Lord Krishna defines karma as 'the force of creation, wherefrom all things have their life,'[1] and warns that 'Because thou art in the bondage of Karma, of the forces of thine own past life; and that which thou, in thy delusion, with a good will dost not want to do, unwillingly thou shalt have to do.'[2] In other words, what a person does in one life influences what has to be done in another.

Hindus believe that karma arises in a causal chain of lives stretching back into the far past. This view of karma is fateful and not a matter of choice. In Eastern eyes, all suffering is caused by karma. The soul takes the sum total of its actions with it after death, and they accompany the next rebirth. The *Bhagavad Gita* states that the earth is 'the world of actions ...' 'All embodied selfs, having here performed good or evil actions, obtain the fruit ...'[3] It tells us that at death the 'soul dropping out of the body, is surrounded on both sides by his own actions, his own pure and meritorious, as also his sinful ones,'[4] and goes on to explain that at birth, 'Coming to one body after another, they [souls] become ripened in their respective ways ... As a blazing lamp shines in a house, even so does consciousness light up bodies. And whatever action he performs, whether good or bad, everything done in a former body must necessarily be enjoyed or suffered. Then that is exhausted, and again other action is accumulated.'[5]

For Hindus, the wheel of rebirth is fixed and unchanging. Karma and past lives determine the circumstances and status of the present life. Hindu society is stratified and the soul must live a particularly good life if it is to achieve a higher status in a future life. Brahmins, the high, priestly caste, have been and always will be Brahmins – unless they accumulate considerable 'negative karma', or until they step off the wheel. Stepping off the wheel is achieved by recognizing that one is, and always has been, part of the divine. To merge with this quality is to achieve 'salvation' or immortality. It is a long process and is rarely achieved in one life.

In the *Bhagavad Gita*, a man, Arjuna, enquires of the god Krishna what happens to a righteous man after death. Krishna replies: 'The man whose devotion has been broken off by death goeth to the regions of the righteous, where he dwells for an immensity of years and is then born again on earth in a pure and fortunate family or even in a family of those who are spiritually illuminated ... Being thus born again he comes in contact with the knowledge which belonged to him in his former body, and from that time he struggles more diligently towards perfection.'[6]

However, the man who has what Krishna describes as a 'dead soul' will not have a good rebirth. This is the man who had insatiable desires and was 'full of deceit, insolence and pride' and whose highest aim was sensual enjoyment. It is this man of whom Krishna says: 'In the vast cycles of life and death I inexorably hurl them down to destruction, these are the lowest of men, cruel and evil, whose soul is hate. Reborn in a lower life, in darkness birth after birth, they come not to me, Arjuna; but they go down the path of hell. And so they will continue, life after life.'[7]

Karma, in the eastern view, appears to be an unending round. Notwithstanding, Hindus do believe that remission of karma is possible. In the Kumbh Mela festival that takes place every twelve years, pilgrims come to bathe in the waters of the Ganges at Allahabad. This is the site of a titanic battle that took place aeons ago between the gods and the demons of Hinduism. They fought over a pitcher containing the nectar of immortality. Where drops of the nectar spilt, the river became holy. Bathing in the river is said to bring *Moksha* or salvation, a release from the round of rebirth. Karma is cleared. Merit karma may also be earned. In a television interview, a policeman on duty at the Kumbh Mela festival said that, whilst he would be too busy to bathe himself, in aiding other people to bathe he would be fulfilling his karma – which he interpreted as duty. He would earn merit from this act. He declared that it was better to have helped two other people than to bathe himself.[8]

Allahabad is also said to be the site where the subterranean Saraswati river merges with the Ganges. This is a symbolic river signifying man's knowledge and learning so the site is an appropriate one to bathe away the ignorance that underlies karma. Whilst immersion in the river does not guarantee release from rebirth, for someone close to obtaining this goal, the act may be the final impetus needed. It may signify the end to rebirth for that particular soul.

Jains too believe that karma can be neutralized. But it requires many lives of unceasing penance to release from previous acts. Ideally, these lives should be lived as a monk. With a 'concentrated mind' a monk can destroy his karma – acquired through acts of both love and hatred – by six acts of penance: Abstaining from destroying life, abstaining from lying, refraining from taking anything not freely given, celibacy, having no personal property and eating only at night. In addition to this, the monk must destroy his illusions, remove obstructions to knowledge, and practise many disciplines and abstinences. Having achieved all this, when his death approaches he must then enter into pure meditation, shut down his mind and his bodily functions, and allow his soul to pass once more into its pure form, in which he 'gains enlightenment and puts an end to all misery'.[9]

For Hindus, Sikhs and Jains, karma is a matter for the individual soul or *Atman*. The *Atman* is divine, part of a celestial energy immanent throughout the universe, and it passes from life to life on its journey to rediscover its origins and to rejoin the divine. For Buddhists, however, the concept is somewhat different. They agree that karma is action followed by reaction, saying: 'Kammic process (kaama-bhava) is the force in virtue of which reaction follows actions, it is the energy that out of a present life, conditions a future life in un-ending sequence.'[10] Where they differ is that most Buddhists do not believe that there is an individual soul that carries karma from life to life, although some Buddhists, especially the Tibetans, surmise that individual mind, or consciousness, continues.

In one 20th-century compilation of ancient *Buddhist Texts,* karma is defined as 'volitional action, which is either wholesome or un-wholesome, it is that which passes in unbroken continuity from one momentary congeries of the *skandhas* to another, either during the life of a person or after his death, until the result of every volitional activity of body, speech or thought, that has been done, is arrived at.'[11] The 'momentary congeries of the *skandhas*' refers to a temporary coming together of the 'psycho-constituents of reality' – form, sensation or feeling, perception, intention and consciousness – that form a 'causal chain' for the experiences of a particular life. However, these constituents are not regarded as a soul or on-going individual identity. They are 'conditioned things' that create 'life events' as a manifestation of karma and then scatter again at death.

Dependent Origination
A 'chain of events' that arises from moment to moment, one thing arising out of another, interconnected but having no independent existence of their own.

Buddhists believe in 'Dependent Origination'. *Vinnana paccaya Nama-rupa* can be translated as 'from consciousness arise name and form', that is to say, everything changes from moment to moment and it is the ego, or self-consciousness, that holds things together with its perceptions. At death the ego dissolves, leaving the five *skandhas* or elements: form, sensations, perceptions, intentions and consciousness. At death, the 'soul' fragments into separate *skandhas*, which can combine and recombine with *skandhas* from other souls. Rather than a single soul reincarnating, mental and physical personality constituents form consciousness. That consciousness, conditioned by ignorance and actions (karma), and motivated by craving, determines the next existence. Karma, in this view, is seeded into the womb of the new mother as a 'soul-aspect' but it is argued that nothing actually passes from body to body, only an impulse.

Paticca samuppada is extremely subtle. It is often defined as the 'chain of causation' that lies behind pain, suffering and rebirth. 'Existence is seen as an interrelated flux of phenomenal events, material and psychical, without any real, permanent, independent existence of their own.'[12] That is, one thing arises out of another that in turn arose out of prior conditions. These things are links in a chain which intertwine but are complete in themselves. Buddhism has no interest in 'first causes' as everything is in a state of becoming. Events happen in a series, one interrelating group producing another, which creates bondage to rebirth due to ignorance of the true state of affairs – that this is only how it *appears to be*. This bondage or chain of causation has twelve stages, the first two of which relate to a previous life and thus explain the present.

According to this view, karma is set in motion when 'faulty thinking', based on ignorance of the nature of man and the nature of reality, causes rebirth. The nature of man is spiritual, the nature of reality an illusion produced by consciousness (mind) or perception.

151

This ignorance leads to 'karmic tendencies' being carried into incarnation. Taking on name and form, that is personal identity, a false sense of ego and separateness are created and the process of individuality begins. The five senses and the objects they perceive lead to illusions as the mind co-ordinates sense impressions and creates its own reality from these. The contact between objects and the five senses leads to sensation, which gives rise to desire, which results in holding onto the object desired.

Chain of Causation behind the Cycle of Existence

1. *Ignorance*
2. *Karmic Predispositions*
3. *Consciousness*
4. *Form and Body*
5. *Five sense organs and the mind*
6. *Contact*
7. *Feeling responses*
8. *Craving*
9. *Grasping for an object (or desire)*
10. *Actions*
11. *Birth*
12. *Old Age and Death*

So, for example, if a man's eyes look at a woman and the sensation is pleasing, his karmic predisposition being towards lust, he will lust after her (if his predisposition was towards sexual indifference, he would ignore her). This desire may lead to 'holding onto' her. Seeking pleasure, he may have the illusion of ownership and of power over her. This creates a bond, or karma, between them and could lead to rebirth. *The Majhima* clearly states:

> *Beings are heirs to their deeds; bearers of their*
> *deeds, and their deeds are the womb out of which*
> *they spring, and through their deeds alone they*
> *must change for the better, remake themselves,*
> *and win liberation from ill.*[13]

This *sounds* as though the karma is carried from life to life on an individual basis. But, a disciple of the Buddha stressed that:

> *To believe the doer of the deed will be the same as*
> *the one who experiences its results (in the next life),*
> *this is the one extreme. To believe that the doer of*
> *the deed, and the one who experiences its results*
> *are two different persons, this is the other extreme.*
> *Both these extremes the Perfect One has avoided*
> *and taught the truth that lies in the middle of both.*[14]

So, it would seem that, from the Buddhist view, whilst karma does transmigrate and has a loose attachment to the new incarnation it is not an entirely individualistic thing.

Notwithstanding, in Tibetan Buddhism there is a much stronger concept of individual reincarnation and personal karma. Tibetan Buddhists refer to mind or consciousness rather than soul, but they nevertheless believe that the thoughts and actions of one life will affect the next. What has gone before governs the next incarnation, which may be into animal or other forms as well as human. Tibetan monks, for example, expect to be reincarnated as dogs if they have not fully conformed to their vows. Such a rebirth does not apply only to monks. Nor does rebirth take place merely on the physical, earth plane. It can occur in other realms depending on karma. As the Venerable Lama Lodo explains:

153

*Because of individual karma ... and the results of
negative and positive actions, there are four different
ways to be reborn ...: from a womb (human being);
from an egg (certain animals); as a result of the
attraction to heat (certain insects); and from
instantaneous transformation (certain gods). This
last example is a result of great merit, but yet not
perfect merit since conflicting emotions still remain.*[15]

When questioned whether the next rebirth could be changed or whether it was an unalterable fact – that is, fate – the Lama replied that it could be changed, 'but only by the force of all the actions that you do now'. He explained that accumulating considerable positive karma would have a favourable effect whilst doing many negative deeds would change it for the worst. To wait until the moment of rebirth would be too late as the karmic process was already in motion.

Most Buddhists see life as fated. That is, it has an appointed course to run – a course conditioned by karma. In the *Questions of King Melinda*, a Chinese Buddhist text dating back to the first or second century AD, the sage Nagasena is questioned by the King about premature death:

'Venerable Nagasena, when beings die, do they all die in fullness of time, or do some die out of due season?'[16]

The sage replies that there is such a thing as death at the due time and such a thing as premature death. Some deaths occur in the fullness of time, others do not. He gives an example of a fruit which is ripe and mature and therefore falls in due season. But he also helps the king to see that some fruits fall because 'they are bored into by worms, some because they are knocked down by a long stick, some because they are blown down by the wind, some because they have become rotten', and that these fruits fall out of due season.

Out of due season may not, however, necessarily be out of due time. The king, with whom he is debating, acknowledges that the soul who dies in the womb, in the first month of life or at an advanced age is dying at the appointed time. So, it would appear, there are no accidents. And yet, the sage goes on to say that there are seven kinds of men for whom time could be said to run out while they still have a portion of their allotted span to run. These are men who starve or who die from thirst, men who are killed by snake bite and those who take poison, men who die from fire or drowning, and those who die from a 'dart' (sword or knife). With the exception of these inadvertent deaths, all deaths are karmic and fall in due season. And yet, Nagasena goes on to say, some of those seven deaths could also be due to retributive karma:

> *But there are some men, O king, who die through*
> *the working of some evil deed or other they have*
> *committed in a former birth. And of these, O king,*
> *whosoever has starved others to death, after having*
> *been himself through many hundreds of thousands*
> *of years tormented by hunger, famished, exhausted,*
> *emaciated and withered of heart, dried up, wasted*
> *away, heated, and all on fire within, will, either as*
> *youth or man or old man, die of hunger too. And that*
> *death will be to him a death at the appointed time ...*[17]

And so on through all the different deaths, each causing exquisite torment to the former tormentor. This tormentor, so it would appear from the text, has a chain of incarnations as an individual soul who reaps the rewards of his previous actions.

155

Tibetan Buddhism and Dissolving Karma

In Tibetan Buddhism it is possible to aid others to dissolve their negative karma, and to work on your own karma in the same way. By practising and expressing compassion, karma is alleviated.

The Tibetan teacher Sogyal Rinpoche speaks in his book on living and dying of how compassion can purify karma through the practices of *phowa* and *tonglen*. *Tonglen*, which means giving and receiving, can be put to work by those who care for the dying or to aid anyone who is suffering pain. It can also be used by those in pain themselves. Sogyal Rinpoche feels that *tonglen* is one of the most useful and powerful of all spiritual practices because it unblocks the heart and purifies the mind. By opening to the truth of the suffering of others, any forces blocking the heart are destroyed as is estrangement or separation from another person. By opening to this loving practice, bitterness and despair are dissolved. '[*Tonglen*] is effective in destroying the self-grasping, self-cherishing, self-absorption of the ego, which is the root of all our suffering and the root of all hard-heartedness.'[18]

Tonglen takes on the suffering of others by identifying with it, drawing it into oneself for transformation, and then breathing out love, compassion, peace and well being to transform the pain. It works for physical pain, mental distress and emotional disturbances, and any other form of suffering. It can also be used with forgiveness. In accepting total responsibility for one's actions, without trying to justify them, acknowledgement is made for what has gone, or been done wrong, and forgiveness requested wholeheartedly. The practice is divided into two parts: breathing in and breathing out. If you want to purify your own karma you need to 'split in two' and become your own best friend. As you breathe in, that best friend opens its heart to encompass all your suffering, hurt and pain with loving compassion. If you are performing Tonglen for someone else, then you open your heart to them and absorb their pain in your loving compassion – which purifies and dissolves it. When breathing out, reconciliation, forgiveness and healing are sent either to yourself or to the other person if you are undertaking the practice on behalf of someone else in particular, or to wherever it is needed if you are working for the greater good of all.

Phowa, which means transferring consciousness, is used to prepare for one's own death and to aid anyone who is dying or has already died. In one form, it is a prayer addressed to whichever deity or spiritual force you associate with truth, wisdom and compassion, accompanied by a visualization and a merging of consciousness with the golden light flowing from the chosen deity, so that this light melts karma. In other forms, the prayer is omitted, moving straight to the experience of union. Done for oneself, this practice prepares for death, so that it becomes automatic at the moment of death to transfer consciousness to the highest possible state and allow the karma to be dissolved. Carried out on behalf of someone who is dying, it aids them in transferring their consciousness. The prayer is:

> *Through your blessing, grace, and guidance,*
> *through the power of the light that streams*
> *from you:*
> *May all my negative karma, destructive*
> *emotions, obscurations, and blockages be*
> *purified and removed.*
> *May I know myself forgiven for all the*
> *harm I may have thought and done,*
> *May I accomplish this profound practice of*
> *phowa, and die a good and peaceful death,*

And through the triumph of my death, may I be
able to benefit all other beings, living or dead.[19]

Whilst it may feel presumptuous to take into oneself the suffering
of others, this is nevertheless a very effective practice that can be
carried out by anyone provided that it is done with compassion and
not with arrogance.

Karma in the West

Karma is not exclusively an Eastern concept. The idea occurred in
ancient Egypt, Greece and Rome; in Judaism and Christianity; and
in Celtic thought. The Celts were such strong believers in rebirth that
they would happily take a pledge to repay a debt in a future life if it
could not be fulfilled in the present.

A belief in karma and karmic consequences does not rely on the
concept of reincarnation. That what has gone before, whether in
one life or many, can create sickness and disease is a universal
belief, as is the concept of a judgement after which the wicked
cease to exist and the good are rewarded by eternal life. That the
actions of the soul whilst on earth played a considerable part in the
Afterlife is a consistent belief in most western religious systems.

Egypt

The Afterlife was a fundamental tenet of life in ancient Egypt.
Indeed, life itself was a preparation for the next world and much of
the religious ritual was concerned with placating the dead or helping them to have a good rebirth – either in the hereafter or into a
new physical body.

In *Egyptian Belief and Modern Thought*, first published in 1878 (but republished by Falcon's Wing Press in 1956), James Bonwick stated that 'The Ritual [Egyptian Book of the Dead] is full of allusions to the doctrine [reincarnation]' ... 'the funeral books show us clearly that resurrection was, in reality, but a renovation, leading to a new existence, a new infancy, and a new youth.' '[The] soul was reborn in order to accomplish a new terrestrial existence under many forms.' He is convinced that the Egyptians believed in karma, going on to say: 'The pampered sensualist returned a beggar; the proud oppressor, a slave; the selfish woman of fashion, a seamstress. A turn of the wheel gave a chance for the development of neglected or abused intelligence and feeling.'

If the incarnating soul had not lived a good life, then it had much to fear. The Egyptian soul, for instance, who faced the Judgement of Osiris after death, had to declare that it had not committed sins such as adultery or greed:

> *Behold me: I am come to you, void of wrong,*
> *without fraud, a harmless one ... I subsist upon*
> *Righteousness ... I have given bread to the*
> *hungry, water to the thirsty, clothes to the naked,*
> *a boat to the shipwrecked ... I am one whose*
> *mouth is pure and whose hands are pure ...*[20]

If the soul could not make such a confession, then it was doomed to extinction. Consumed by the Eater of Souls, it existed no more – although some tomb paintings show such a soul passing into the body of an animal or undergoing terrible torments. If it could pass the Judgement, then the soul travelled on through the other world, aided by the correct amulets and incantations to open the Gates.

Advice on living life to the best advantage, and so as not to accrue karma, was given by the sage Ptah-Hotep: 'Do nothing to excess ... A man whose heart is powerful and stable, a man who is not the slave of his belly's demands – that man can hope to hear God.'[21] This man would pass the Judgement of Osiris which weighed the heart of the deceased against the feather of Maat, truth or, more properly, balance.

The French Egyptologist Christian Jacq found an intriguing tale of magic which shows that the idea of return to earth to carry out a karmic intention was no stranger to the Egyptians. In it, Siusire, son of Setna, successfully takes up a challenge laid down by an Ethiopian magician to read the contents of a sealed envelope – clearly part of a larger karmic power struggle that went on throughout ancient Egypt's history. Angered at Siusire's success, the magician makes four porters and a litter out of wax. Muttering incantations, he infuses them with life and orders them to bring the *ka* or astral body of the Pharaoh to Ethiopia. Here the King is given five hundred lashes and much magic has to be invoked to save him. A great magical battle then takes place between the god Horus and the magician, who is narrowly defeated when he turns himself into a bird. A bird-catcher is about to stab the magician-bird when the magician's mother intervenes to beg for mercy. They both promise not to return to Egypt for 1500 years. It seems that Siusire was an incarnation of Horus, who had himself died 1500 years earlier but returned to overcome the magician. It was his karma to save Egypt twice – as he had previously overcome the nefarious plans of his wicked uncle Seth to take over the country. Once the task was accomplished a second time, the manuscript tells us that Siusire simply vanished before the eyes of his father and Pharaoh.[22]

Greece

Greece inherited many Egyptian beliefs as the great philosophers travelled to Egypt for initiation, but it had its own strand of teachings too. The concept of karma underlay the Greek perception of rebirth and, with the spread of the Roman Empire, passed down into Christianity through an infusion of Jewish and Romano-Greek thought. Many of the ancient Greeks strongly believed in both the afterlife and in reincarnation. In reincarnation, the soul was given a new body in accordance with its deeds in a former life. So, in his play *Timaeus*, the philosopher Plato sets out the fate of men as he sees it. Not all of them will come back as human beings:

> *He who lived well during his appointed time was*
> *to return and dwell in his native star, and there*
> *he would have a blessed and congenial existence.*
> *But if he failed in attaining this, at the second*
> *birth he would pass into a woman, and if, when*
> *in that state of being, he did not desist from evil,*
> *he would continually be changed into some brute*
> *who resembled him in the evil nature which he*
> *had acquired, and would not cease from his toils*
> *and transformations.*[23]

Timaeus goes on to say that birds were created out of 'lightminded men' and 'wild pedestrian animals' evolved from men who had no philosophy, whilst the 'most entirely ignorant and senseless of all evolved into the creatures of the sea.'

In Greek belief, the departed soul went to Hades where it spent time in one of several realms according to the nature of its former deeds. From there, after sufficient preparation, it was given the cup of forgetfulness and moved into a new physical body on earth. That body too was conditional upon what had gone before. Nevertheless, Plato warned, through his rendition of the last discourse of Socrates, that it is not only the words and deeds of a departing soul that can influence the next life – whether in Hades or on earth. The words uttered by those around a dying man can also have their effect. Speaking of his friend and follower Crito, who was much troubled at the thought that Socrates was about to drink the poisoned cup and who had not entirely taken on board Socrates' assurance that his soul was immortal and would leave his body at death, Socrates says:

> *I would not have him sorrow at my hard lot, or*
> *say at the burial, Thus we lay out Socrates, or*
> *Thus we follow him to the grave or bury him; for*
> *be well assured, my dear Crito, that false words*
> *are not only evil in themselves, but they infect the*
> *soul with evil.*[24]

The idea that the last words a soul heard could change the course of its passage through the afterlife is one which Tibetan Buddhism shares. Monks are carefully prepared for their demise and rituals are conducted to carry their souls through the Bardo states that follow – states which bear a remarkable resemblance to the descriptions given in Egyptian tomb paintings and papyri relating to the afterlife and to the Greek accounts of the soul's passage through Hades.

Plato's ideas were incorporated into a philosophy known as neo-platonism. Neo-platonist ideas wove down through the centuries carrying with them themes of rebirth and karma. They occurred and reoccurred, subtly influencing many religions and sects including Christianity and Sufism.

Judaism

Judaism bridges western and near-eastern thought. The concept of *mazal* is usually translated 'luck' or 'fortune' but can also be seen as fate: what is written. So the aphorism *mazal toff* is usually seen to mean 'good luck', but a clearer translation could be 'good fate'. A man has to do what is allotted to him, which could be said to be his karma. This fate is, however, apportioned to him by his God to whom retribution for wrong doing belongs. This fate is something more than personal karma. It belongs to the people as a whole and so is an example of racial or tribal karma, which overrides the purely personal level. According to the Law of Moses the Jews belong to their God and he has total control over them. In Deuteronomy, Moses, as the spokesman of this God, warns:

> *If you do not observe and fulfil all the law ... then*
> *the Lord will strike you and your descendants*
> *with unimaginable plagues, malignant and*
> *persistent, and with sickness, persistent and*
> *severe. He will bring upon you once again all the*
> *diseases of Egypt which you dread, and they will*
> *cling to you ... until you are destroyed ... The Lord*
> *will scatter you among all peoples from one end*
> *of the earth to the other ... Among those nations*
> *you will find no peace, no rest for the sole of your*
> *foot. Then the Lord will give you an unquiet*
> *mind, dim eyes, and failing appetite. Your life will*
> *hang continually in suspense, fear will beset you*
> *night and day, and you will find no security all*
> *your life long.*[25]

However, as part of this covenant made by God with his people, they are also offered a positive outcome if they obey him, and also the possibility of forgiveness and restitution should they, or their descendants, turn away and then repent:

> *If you turn back to him and obey him heart and soul in all that I command you this day, then the Lord your God will show you compassion and restore your fortunes. He will gather you again from all the countries to which he has scattered you. Even though he were to banish you to the four corners of the world, the Lord your God will gather you from there, from there he will fetch you home ... and when you turn back to the Lord your God with all your heart and soul, he will again rejoice over you and be good to you.*[26]

Judaic law can be seen as dealing with several kinds of karma – albeit in one life. In Leviticus, Moses passes on the Lord's words:

> *When one man strikes another and kills him, he shall be put to death. Whoever strikes a beast and kills it shall make restitution, life for life. When one man injures and disfigures his fellow countryman, it shall be done to him as he has done; fracture for fracture, eye for eye, tooth for tooth; the injury and disfigurement that he has inflicted upon another shall in turn be inflicted upon him.*[27]

This is 'boomerang karma' at work. What a man does, how he acts, comes back to him with exactitude. Judaic law also sets out with clarity the actions that are required to acquire 'merit karma' and a just reward:

> *At the end of every third year you shall bring out*
> *all the tithe of your produce for that year and*
> *leave it in your settlements so that the Levites, ...*
> *aliens, orphans and widows ... may come and eat*
> *their fill. If you do this the Lord your God will*
> *bless you in everything to which you set your*
> *hand. At the end of every seventh year you shall*
> *make a remission of debts ... everyone who holds*
> *a pledge shall remit the pledge of anyone indebted*
> *to him ... There will never be any poor among you*
> *if only you obey ... [and] the Lord your God will*
> *bless you with great prosperity ... When one of*
> *your countrymen ... becomes poor, do not be*
> *hard-hearted or close fisted ... Be open-handed*
> *towards him and lend him on pledge as much as*
> *he needs. See that you do not harbour iniquitous*
> *thoughts when you find that the seventh year, the*
> *year of remission is near, and look askance at*
> *your needy countryman and give him nothing. If*
> *you do, he will appeal to the Lord against you and*
> *you will be found guilty of sin. Give freely to him*
> *and do not begrudge him your bounty, because it*
> *is for this very bounty that the Lord your God will*
> *bless you in everything that you do or undertake.*[28]

In a modern Hebrew prayer book, obtainable anywhere in Israel for a few shekels, a very ancient prayer is set out. This prayer is recited each night before going to sleep. It offers, and asks for, forgiveness of sins not only in the present life but also in a past life:

Master of the universe, I hereby forgive anyone
who angered or antagonized me or who sinned
against me – whether against my body, my
property, my honour, or anything of mine;
whether he did so accidentally, wilfully,
carelessly, or purposely; whether through speech,
deed, thought, or notion; whether in this
transmigration or another transmigration –
I forgive. May no man be punished because of me.
May it be your will my G-d and the G-d of my
forefathers, that I may sin no more. Whatever
sins I have done before you, may you blot out in
your abundant mercies, but not through suffering
or bad illnesses. May the expression of my mouth
and the thoughts of my heart find favour before
you my Rock and my Redeemer.[29]

This prayer quite clearly sets out the possibility of boomerang karma, that is, actions being punished by suffering or illness but requests that grace should operate in this respect. It also asks pardon for thoughts as well as deeds, knowingly or unknowingly committed, and seeks to release from karmic consequences both the doer and the 'done-against' in this respect.

Whilst there is no specific mention in the Old Testament of karmic consequences in another life, there are many references to karma affecting a future life in the equally ancient oral tradition, the *Talmud*, and in the much more esoteric *Kabala*. Kabalistic wisdom warns that:

If a man be niggardly either in a financial or a
spiritual regard, giving nothing of his money to

the poor, or not imparting of his knowledge to the
ignorant, he shall be punished by transmigration
into a woman.[30]

Kabalists see the Kabala as underlying all knowledge and all religions. It came first and had a profound effect upon world thinking. In the kabalistic view, transmigration and rebirth are a natural progression for the individual soul and for the cosmic soul as it seeks to evolve.

The Apocrypha

The Apocrypha is a body of writings found between the Old and New Testaments in the Christian bible. However, it is not part of the orthodox Jewish canon, being a series of writings in Greek mainly intended for Jews who were in exile in Egypt. The prophet Ezra was a captive of the king of Persia when his God spoke to him. His words form the books of Esdras in *The Apocrypha*. Like all prophets he has a warning of retribution for the wicked and ungodly people around him. But Ezra makes promises too on behalf of his God. He tells his people that if they obey the law, care for their children, bury the unburied, etc, then they will not need to be 'anxious when the time of trouble and hardship comes; others shall lament and be sad, but you shall have happiness and plenty ...'[31] The mysteries of human destiny, and collective karma, are revealed to Ezra in a dream. An angel tells him how evil goes back to Adam:

> *The evil about which you ask me has been sown,*
> *but its reaping has not yet come. Until the crop*
> *of evil has been reaped as well as sown, until the*
> *ground where it was sown has vanished, there*
> *will be no room for the field which has been sown*

with the good. A grain of the evil seed was sown
in the heart of Adam from the first; how much
godlessness has it produced already! How much
more will it produce before the harvest! Reckon
this up; if one grain of evil seed has produced so
great a crop of godlessness, how vast a harvest
will there be when good seeds beyond number
have been sown.[32]

In other words, both group and collective karma are operating here. The effect is cumulative and the 'evil' or 'bad karma' has to be worked off before the 'good karma' can take effect. When Ezra asks about the fate of individual men, particularly those who have gone before, the reply is: 'I will compare the judgement to a circle: the latest will not be too late, nor the earliest too early.' This judgement is clearly described:

Then the Most High shall be seen on the judgement-
seat, and there shall be an end of all pity and
patience. Judgement alone shall remain, truth shall
stand firm and faithfulness be strong ... open
payment [shall] be made; good deeds shall awake
and wicked deeds shall not be allowed to sleep.
Then the place of torment shall appear and over
against it the place of rest; the furnace of hell shall
be displayed, and on the opposite side the paradise
of delight ... Every individual will be held
responsible for his own wickedness or goodness.[33]

According to Ezra, therefore, no matter how much karma was inherited, it was still up to each man to live righteously and to create for himself the conditions whereby he could gain eternal life.

The Apocrypha also contains *The Wisdom of Solomon*. In this wisdom text, the soul says: 'As a soul I was born to excellence, and a noble soul fell to my lot; or rather, I myself was noble, and I entered into an unblemished body.'[34] This verse is often quoted as pertaining to reincarnation but it may simply point to a belief in the pre-existence of the soul which, having been with God, was deemed to be pure rather than having good karma.

Gnostic Christianity

Gnostic Christianity flourished for the first four hundred years after Jesus' death. Gnosis means *knowledge* and the gnostics believed in direct perception and understanding of God. Gnostic Christianity was mystical and incorporated ideas from both Judaism and Greek philosophy. Many of the early Christian bishops were gnostics and several taught reincarnation and karma. Most had studied neo-platonist and other Greek teachings. St Clement of Alexandria (AD 150–220), for instance, wrote that: 'Philolaus, the Pythagorean, taught that the soul was flung into the body as a punishment for the misdeeds it had committed, and his opinion was confirmed by the most ancient of the prophets.'[35] Meanwhile, Origen, one of the most prominent of the early church fathers, asked: 'Is it not more in conformity with reason that every soul for certain mysterious reasons (I speak now according to the opinion of Pythagoras and Plato and Empedocles ...) is introduced into a body, and introduced according to its deserts and former actions? Is it not rational that souls should be introduced into bodies, in accordance with their merits and previous deeds, and that those who have used their bodies in doing the utmost possible good should have a right to bodies endowed with qualities superior to the bodies of others?'[36]

In *The Gospel of Peace of Jesus Christ*, a Gnostic Gospel translated from original Aramaic texts written in the first century after Christ's death, the resurrected Jesus points out to the sick how their condition arises out of their former actions: 'I tell you truly, great and many are your sins. Many years have you yielded to the enticings of Satan. You have been gluttonous, winebibbers and gone-a-whoring, and your past debts have multiplied. And now you must repay them, and payment is difficult and hard.'[37] The payment is immediate, but is open to grace and forgiveness ... The sick are advised to wait seven days until the Sabbath and then go with 'humble and obedient heart' before their Heavenly Father so that he may forgive them their sins and all past debts'.

The idea of a record of all good and evils deeds is also an ancient one, appearing in many cultures. In this Gnostic Gospel Jesus goes on to declare: 'Happy are those that persevere to the end, for the devils of Satan write all your evil deeds in a book, in the book of your body and your spirit ... there is not one sinful deed, but it is written, even from the beginning of the world, before our Heavenly Father ... And when you come before the face of God, the devils of Satan bear witness against you with your deed, and God sees your sins written in the book of your body and of your spirit ... [But if you continue to repent, God] frees you from the clutches of Satan and from suffering ... Long life does he give you, and you shall never see disease.'[38] The Angel of God then records the good deeds done and the former sinner is rewarded with everlasting life. For the writer of this text, purported to be the disciple John, karmic reward and punishment are a combined effort by God and Satan. Later in the same text the listeners are warned: 'Commit not whoredom, by night or by day, for the whoremonger is like a tree whose sap runs out from its trunk. And that tree will be dried up before its time, nor will it ever bear fruit. Therefore, go not a-whoring, lest Satan dry up your body, and the Lord make your seed unfruitful.'[39] This text, contemporary with the New Testament, is one of several hundred accounts originally forming part of the canon of the early Christian church but banned at a Council of Nicea two centuries later for reasons that had more to do with Church politics than spiritual authenticity.

In Gnostic Christianity, karma created the circumstances of the next incarnation. After undergoing terrible torments and retribution in the between-life state, robbers, thieves and men of 'overweening pride' are first handed the cup of forgetfulness and then are cast into: 'a lame, halt and blind body,' for instance. A curser is cast into a body 'which will spend its time continually troubled in its mind'. But a worst fate is reserved for a man who has 'persistently done good' and yet not been initiated into the mysteries. After he has been through purification in the afterlife, 'Thereafter there cometh a receiver of the little Saboath ... He himself bringeth a cup filled with thoughts and wisdom and soberness is in it; [and] he handeth it to the soul. And they cast it into a body which can neither sleep nor forget because of the cup of soberness which hath been handed unto it; but it will whip its heart persistently to question about the mysteries of the Light until it find them.'[40]

The *Gospel of Thomas* is one of the gnostic texts discovered at Nag Hammadi in Egypt. It is a collection of teachings translated from Greek into Coptic and preserved by the Egyptian church. It is closely related to the source document drawn upon by Matthew and Luke (writers of gospels which are accepted by the orthodox church) and is believed to date back to the first or second century, some scholars asserting it was written only a few decades after Jesus' death. Many scholars believe that the *Gospel of Thomas* preserves most closely the actual words of Jesus. It purports to be 'the secret sayings which the living Jesus spoke'. In other words, it is the collection of esoteric or hidden teachings given to the inner circle of disciples.

Whilst the *Gospel of Thomas* does not explicitly mention karma, Jesus does tell his followers: 'Grapes are not harvested from thorns, nor are figs gathered from thistles, for they do not produce fruit. A good man brings forth good from his storehouse, an evil man brings forth evil things from his evil storehouse, which is in his heart, and says evil things. For out of the abundance of the heart he brings forth evil things.'[41] As this gospel is a 'guidebook to achieving eternal life' and returning the soul to its primordial, pristine state of oneness, it is sensible to suppose that the 'storehouse' concerned is a karmic one, whether from one life or many – most gnostics being believers in reincarnation.

Orthodox Christianity

Within the New Testament itself, there are many remnants of similar teaching. St Paul, in his letter to the Romans, reveals 'God's way of righting wrongs'. He warns that a 'divine retribution' will fall from heaven upon all the 'godless wickedness of men'. For Paul, the cardinal sin is not acknowledging God. All other sins stem from this and sin can also be called karma. However, Paul sees sin, or karma, as arising out of the freedom which God has given to men to do what they will:

> *He has given them up to their own depraved*
> *reason. This leads them to break all rules of*
> *conduct. They are filled with every kind of*
> *injustice, mischief, rapacity and malice; they are*
> *one mass of envy, murder, rivalry, treachery, and*
> *malevolence; whisperers and scandal-mongers ...*

> *insolent, arrogant and boastful; they invent*
> *new kinds of mischief, they show no loyalty to*
> *parents, no conscience, no fidelity to their*
> *plighted word; they are without natural affection*
> *and without pity ...*[42]

The consequences are dire:

> *In the rigid obstinacy of your heart you are*
> *laying up for yourself a store of retribution for*
> *the day of retribution when God's just judgement*
> *will be revealed and he will pay every man for*
> *what he has done ... There will be trouble and*
> *distress for every human being who is an*
> *evil-doer.*[43]

In Paul's eyes, the only way to overcome the possibility of retribution is to die to the old self and be 'resurrected in Christ'. To rise above what Paul calls the 'lower nature' and move into the spiritual nature. As he says:

> *A man reaps what he sows. If he sows seed in the*
> *field of his lower nature, he will reap from it a*
> *harvest of corruption, but if he sows in the field*
> *of the Spirit, the Spirit will bring him a harvest of*
> *eternal life. So let us never tire of doing good, for*
> *if we do not slacken our efforts we shall in due*
> *time reap our harvest.*[44]

That harvest is eternal life.

The notion of harvest was a common one, indicating something coming to fruition, linking to what has been referred to as 'the fruitage of lives', or karma. In Luke's rendering of the teaching given in the *Gospel of Thomas*, Jesus says:

> *There is no such thing as a good tree producing*
> *worthless fruit, nor yet a worthless tree*
> *producing good fruit. For each tree is known by*
> *its own fruit ... A good man produces good fruit*
> *from the store of good within himself; and an evil*
> *man from evil which produces evil. For the words*
> *that the mouth utters come from the overflowing*
> *of the heart.*[45]

Jesus himself gave many teachings which could be called karmic. In the body of teachings that were gathered together and became known as the Sermon on the Mount, he expands upon Jewish law saying:

> *You have learned that our forefathers were told:*
> *'Do not commit murder; anyone who commits*
> *murder must be brought to judgement.' But*
> *what I tell you is this: Anyone who nurses*
> *anger against his brother must be brought to*
> *judgement. If he abuses his brother he must*
> *answer for it to the court; if he sneers at him he*
> *will have to answer for it in the fires of hell.*[46]

In other words, it is what a man holds in his heart that determines the reward or retribution that will come to him and which will influence the future course of his life – or afterlife.

Jesus goes on to say that if a man recalls that his brother has a grievance against him, then he should go and make his peace with his brother before offering up a sacrifice. In other words, at each moment in time, the karma should be cleared. It should not be left to accumulate. That a thought is as significant as a deed is made clear in the statement: 'You have learned they [the forefathers] were told: "Do not commit adultery." But what I tell you is this: If a man looks on a woman with a lustful eye, he has already committed adultery with her in his heart.'[47]

In the same body of teaching, Jesus reverses the 'eye for an eye' edict, saying 'Do not set yourself against the man who wrongs you. If someone slaps you on the right cheek, turn and offer him your left.' He specifically instructs: 'Pass no judgement, and you will not be judged. For as you judge others, so you will yourselves be judged, and whatever measure you deal out to others will be dealt back to you.'[48] This is an example of 'boomerang karma' at work. He sums up the Law as 'Always treat others as you would like them to treat you.' That a karmic account is kept is clear from Jesus' statement: 'There is not a thoughtless word that comes from men's lips but they will have to account for it on the day of judgement.'[49]

An example of reaching karmic equilibrium, how one thing will be balanced by another, is given in the teaching:

> *How blest are you who now go hungry, your*
> *hunger shall be satisfied.*
> *How blest are you who weep now, you shall*
> *laugh ...*
> *But alas for you who are rich; you shall have had*
> *your time of happiness.*

*Also for you who are well-fed now; you shall go
hungry.
Also for you who laugh now; you shall mourn
and weep ...*[50]

But the most direct mention of karma – and of reincarnation – is in the story of the man who was born blind, reported in St John's gospel. St John's gospel is the most mystical of the four, clearly showing the influence of Greek thought. His gospel is the closest to gnosticism – and indeed the gospel opens with the statement: 'In the beginning was the word' or gnosis.

*As he went on his way Jesus saw a man blind
from his birth. His disciples put the question:
'Rabbi, who sinned, this man or his parents? Why
was he born blind?' 'It is not that this man or his
parents sinned,' Jesus answered; 'he was born
blind so that God's power might be displayed in
curing him ...*[51]

In asking if the man had done something to cause him to be born blind, the disciples and the onlookers are implying that he lived before his birth, and that his blindness could be a punishment for some previous event – in other words, his karma. Jesus' answer, however, brings out an important aspect of karma. The blindness is part of the greater purpose. It could be seen as redemptive karma. Richmond Lattimore's modern translation renders that sentence: 'Neither he nor his parents sinned, it was so that the workings of God might be made manifest in him. We must do the work of him who sent us while it is day.'[52] In other words, it was the man's karmic purpose to be born blind so that he would be available to be healed when the time came, but, at the same time, it could be said to have been his fate or destiny.

Theosophy and Modern Esotericism

In the modern esoteric view, karma is a continuous process working towards a balance. The rewards, or otherwise, of actions may be reaped in the next moment or at any time in the future. However, it is not simply a matter of 'reward' or 'punishment'. It is part of an on-going rounding-out of experience. So, a soul may deliberately choose a difficult incarnation in order to learn or experience a given set of circumstances. Equally, a soul who feels a need to make reparation, could well choose a life of service or to take on some of the collective karma of humanity.

Madame Blavatsky, founder of Theosophy, believed that life was particularly difficult for Europeans because they were taught to believe that the circumstances of their life were the result of 'blind hazard' rather than karma. But, in her view, only karma and reincarnation can explain those circumstances. It was the only thing that explained 'inequalities of birth and fortune, of intellect and capacities ...' For Blavatsky knowledge of karma was what kept one from cursing life and the creator in the face of the helplessness experienced 'when one sees honour paid to fools and profligates, on whom fortune has heaped her favours by mere privilege of birth, and their nearest neighbour, with all his intellect and noble virtues – far more deserving in every way – perishing of want and for lack of sympathy'.[53]

But she warned against blaming everything on karma because the reincarnated man had a part in what was created as well as the patterns he carried from other lives:

177

Karma creates nothing, nor does it design. It is man who plans and creates causes, and Karmic Law adjusts the effects, which adjustment is not an act, but universal harmony, tending ever to resume its original position, like a bough, which, bent down too forcibly, rebounds with corresponding vigour ... Karma has never sought to destroy intellectual and individual liberty ... Karma is an Absolute and Eternal Law in the World of Manifestation.[54]

For Theosophists, the germs of that old life are carried in the Permanent Mental Atom, a particle that travels with the astral body after death and then incarnates once again, but which can also pass down through the family. One of her followers defined the Permanent Mental Atom as 'a collector of the fruitage of lives ... [a] storehouse of the acquired tendencies of lives.'[55]

Annie Besant developed the concept of karma still further, saying: 'the knowledge of karma ... removed human thought and desire from the region of arbitrary happenings to the realm of law, and thus places man's future under his own control in proportion to the amount of his knowledge.'[56] According to Besant, karma is the law of causation '– law eternal, changeless, invariable, inviolable, law which can never be broken, existing in the nature of things'[57] and, as such, can be modified. She points out that whilst some 'uninformed people' might say: 'You must not interfere with his karma,' in actual fact, karma, being a natural law like gravitation, for instance, can be neutralized, circumvented or turned aside 'exactly according to our knowledge of its nature and working, and the forces at our disposal. Karma is no more "sacred" than any other natural law'.[58] She defines a natural law as 'a sequence of conditions'. Left to themselves, the conditions will take a natural course. But if intelligence and knowledge are applied, then the natural law is set aside.

To Annie Besant, karma was not an inevitable destiny imposed from outside. She believed that, by having knowledge of their karma, a man or woman could change his or her nature. She insisted that 'karma is not a power which crushes, but a statement of conditions out of which invariable results accrue.'[59] Nevertheless, given insights and intention, that inevitable outcome could be amended by the creation of new habits and the implementation of thought, desire and action in a new way. These new habits would be put to work on the physical, emotional and mental levels. If change could not be brought about fully, then adapting to circumstances was recommended, especially if they could be brought round to advantage. Besant saw the working of karma as partly fate and partially free will. She said:

> We are partly compelled and partly free. We
> must work amid conditions which we have
> created, but we are free within them to work
> upon them ... we ... are inherently free but we can
> only work in and through the thought-nature, the
> desire-nature, and the physical nature, which we
> have created; these are our materials and our
> tools, and we can have none other till we make
> these anew.[60]

It was her contention that there were many strands of karma that interwove throughout life, some good, some bad.

Notwithstanding, in *A Study in Karma* it is obvious that much of the karma Annie Besant spoke of is what would be regarded as

'boomerang' or retributive karma. She specifically says that hereditary and congenital diseases are 'reactions from past misdeeds' and
that 'a "bad heredity" is the reaction from wrong activities in the
past.' In speaking of karma as 'perfect justice' she says: 'Extreme
cruelty inflicted on the helpless – on heretics, on children, on animals – reacts on inquisitors, on brutal parents and teachers, on
vivisectors, as physical deformity, more or less revolting and
extreme, according to the nature and extent of the cruelty.' For her,
seemingly, deformity and disability in the present life are inevitably
linked to 'misdemeanors' in a past life. Nevertheless, she does also
say that the motive behind acts will affect the consequences, even
when that motive is 'intellectually misdirected'. So, for instance, if a
vivisector carries out the act in order to save others from the ravages
of disease, then the karmic consequences will be somewhat different: 'Hence we may find a person born deformed, with a gentle and
patient character, showing that in a past life he strove to see the
right and did the wrong.' On the other hand, where 'lust for power
and indifference to the pain of others have mingled their baleful
influences with the infliction of cruelty, there will be found also a
mental and emotional twist.'[61]

Madame Blavatsky and Annie Besant had a profound influence on
the esoteric groups of the twentieth century. Many of the groups
seeking metaphysical understanding, and a number of the individuals concerned with opening up awareness, were grounded in their
teachings. However, the view of karma has, in the century following
the setting up of Theosophy, evolved somewhat. The modern esoteric view of karma is much less deterministic and retributive. The
soul is recognized as a spiritual being who is on a human journey of
evolution, and yet at the same time remains part of the greater
whole. A viewpoint which considerably opens up the idea of cause
and effect. As Ruth White, a modern karmic teacher, puts it: 'Karma

and reincarnation give space for compassion and a deeper under-standing of the process of human evolution'.[62]

Rudolf Steiner and Anthroposophy

Whilst Theosophy and other Western metaphysical schools turned to Buddhism and the East for inspiration, Rudolph Steiner (1861–1925) was a Christian occultist who sought to re-establish a spiritual science that incorporated Christianity. Steiner began his spiritual search by joining the Theosophical Society and he took on some of its ideas, but he gave much more weight to the Christ spirit, whom Steiner believed had become the Lord of Karma.

Steiner envisaged spiral evolution for the human soul. According to him, consciousness was evolving upwards (fulfilling cosmic karma) and, although a certain amount of repetitive experience would be required, on the whole the soul was moving ever onwards. Steiner's fundamental teaching is that of reincarnation as a basis of soul-learning and it is his suggestion that, for instance, those souls who incarnate into a handicapped or disadvantaged body may well be evolved souls who return with the specific intention of allowing others to learn through caring for that body (that is, they practise redemptive karma).

For Steiner, thought was the creator of matter and the world responded to a set of spiritual laws or principles. He postulated that a soul would make use of factors such as heredity and the collective unconscious or racial memory in its incarnations, but would not be governed by these. So, thought would create both the physical body and the environment around it. It would also form a matrix which would interpenetrate the physical body and the more subtle bodies that survive death. In this way, memories and karma could be carried from life to life and into the spiritual planes where they would be held in the Akashic Record (a spiritual record of all that had gone before). This matrix would then be moulded by the new ego – which Steiner thought of as a spiritual force rather than a personality-based ego – to form the next incarnation experience.

Steiner postulated three types of memory, linked to the subtle bodies that the soul inhabited. The day-to-day memory fell away after death unless it had been connected to the etheric rather than the physical body. The universal memory held personal memories which passed into the Akashic Record and became part of the soul memory of the planet. Finally, memory could pass into the astral body which existed after the physical and the etheric bodies had passed away. It was through the astral body that memories of other lives could be accessed and karma could work itself out.

Steiner saw one further memory unit, that of the 'I' which preserved karma and previous life memory. This was earth-based rather than spiritual because it recorded experiences whilst in incarnation, and held memories of karmic responsibilities. There was, however, a complementary 'spiritual-I'. If the 'spiritual-I' was awakened in an incarnation, it would combine with the memories and intention of the 'earth-I' and bring to mind spiritual purpose. This would awaken the ability to aid humanity's evolution.

To Steiner, a man could 'become one with his fate', that is, he could merge with his karmic intention. It was Steiner's understanding that: 'However the blows of fate may have fallen, whether bringing good or ill – we are now what we are now through all the hard and kind blows of fate: we are in the end nothing but the result of this fate of ours ... and in making this reflection we grow into our fate.'[63] The soul became what it was meant to be.

Steiner taught that certain souls, such as the prophet Elijah (whom Steiner believed became John the Baptist, the Renaissance painter Raphael, and finally the German romantic poet Novalis), incarnated again and again to help humanity evolve through their teachings – that is, they practised redemptive karma. These 'great spirits' were responding to an evolutionary rhythm which could be said to be cosmic karma in action.

In a series of lectures on karma given in 1910, Steiner laid out his karmic understanding of how the personal karma of individuals interwove with the karma of large groups and ultimately with the collective. To him, karma was much more than mere abstract cause and effect. It was a 'teaching which not only tells us how different things in the world relate to one another, but will make our lives more satisfying and rich.'[64] The richness arose from becoming one with soul intention and karmic purpose.

Steiner also taught that a cosmic battle was taking place between the forces of light and the forces of darkness. First one would be in the ascendancy, then the other. This was a fundamental part of both human and cosmic evolution. He spoke of 'higher beings', Lucifer and Ahriman who, just like humanity, were seeking to evolve. The two could aid each other but they could also be at cross purposes. Ahriman's influence could be positive but was equally likely to involve illusion and deception, particularly at a spiritual level. Lucifer's influence worked through the astral body in the area of feelings, instincts and passions. However, neither of these forces was solely 'bad', the two were a counter-point to each other, each bringing up different karma. It was Steiner's contention that some souls would be particularly open to these forces (or the beings that were attuned to them) acting through them, and so could become involved in the cosmic progression but, at the same time, the soul's karma would be 'fructified by the general karma that streams through the world'. This would ultimately lead towards spiritual evolution for the whole.

APPENDIX

Edgar Cayce

Edgar Cayce was an American psychic. During his life he gave over 15,000 psychic readings. More than 2,500 of those referred to past lives and many were devoted to the karmic cause of illness. A devout Christian, Cayce nevertheless came to believe in reincarnation from the information he produced when in trance. He saw himself as Pythagoras and several early spiritual teachers. Cayce worked in a trance state which he had learned during a past life as a Persian physician. Wounded in a battle, he had been left to die. Without food or water for three days, he was in agony. By a supreme effort, he detached his consciousness from his body; an ability that stood him in good stead in his current life as he could put himself into trance at will. Cayce first went into trance to find the cause of a throat condition that literally left him speechless. If Cayce did not do the work he was intended to do – his readings – then his throat closed up and he could not speak.

Cayce stated that he had accrued karma as a strong-willed and sensual Egyptian priest who broke his vow of celibacy in order to create 'a perfect child'. He was reborn twice as John Bainbridge, once in the 17th century and then again in the 18th century. Both men had a lustful disposition and were restless and unhappy. Cayce said that he had had to undergo those lives as he needed to know extremes before he could help others. At the end of the second John Bainbridge life, he gave his own life to save that of another. Cayce felt that his current lifetime was a 'test for his soul'. His work gave him an opportunity to overcome the pride, materialism and sensuality of his past lives and to serve humankind selflessly.

BIBLIOGRAPHY

Bibliography

Besant, A *A Study in Karma* The Theosophist Office, Madras, no date.

Blavatsky, HP *The Secret Doctrine* The Theosophical Publishing House, London, 1928 edition (3 vols).

Candlish, Alan *The Revised Waites Compendium of Natal Astrology* Penguin Arkana, London, 1990 (out of print).

Cerminara, Gina *Many Mansions* New American Library, NY, 1950.

Conze, Edward (ed) *Buddhist Texts through the Ages* Bruno Cassirer, Oxford, 1954.

Forman, Werner and Quirke, Stephen *Hieroglyphs and the Afterlife in Ancient Egypt* BCA, London, 1996.

Hall, Judy *Hands Across Time* Findhorn Press, Inverness, 1997.

– *Deja Who? A Fresh Look at Past Lives* Findhorn Press, Inverness, 1998.

– *Karmic Connections* The Wessex Astrologer, Bournemouth, 2001.

– *Patterns of the Past* The Wessex Astrologer, Bournemouth, 2000.

– *Principles of Past Life Therapy* Thorsons, London, 1996.

– *The Way of Reincarnation* Thorsons, London, 2001.

– *The Hades Moon* Samuel Weiser, Maine, 1998.

Head, Joseph and Cranston, SL *Reincarnation: An East West Anthology* The Julian Press, New York, 1961.

Jacq, Christian *Magic and Mystery in Ancient Egypt* Souvenir Press, London, 1998.

– *The Black Pharaoh* Simon & Schuster, London, 1999.

Jones, Kathy *Breast Cancer: Hanging on by a red thread* Ariadne Publications, 56 Whiting Road, Glastonbury BA6 8HR, 1998.

Lattimore, Richmond *The New Testament* JM Dent, London, 1998.

Lodo, Venerable Lama *Bardo Teachings: The Way of Death and Rebirth* Snow Lion Publications, Ithaca, NY, 1982.

Mascaro, Juan *The Bhagavad Gita* Penguin Classics, London, 1962.

Max Muller, F (ed) *Sacred Books of the East* Motital Banarsidess, Dehli, 1965.

Mead, GRS *Pistis Sophia* Kessinger Publishing, Kila, USA, no date.

Motoyama, Dr Hiroshi *Karma and Reincarnation* Piatkus, London, 1992.

Newton, Michael *Journey of Souls* Llewellyn Publications, Minnesota, 1999.

Paticca Samuppada Piyadassi: Dependent Origination Thera Buddhist Publication Society, Kandy, 1959.

Plato *Dialogues of Plato, Volumes 1 and 2* trans. Benjamin Jowett, Sphere, London, 1970.

– *Last Days of Socrates* trans. Hugh Tredennick, Penguin Classics, London, 1961.

Prokofieff, Sergei O *Eternal Individuality: Towards a Karmic Biography of Novalis* trans. Simon Blaxland de Lange, Temple Lodge Publishing, London, 1992.

Robinson, James (ed) *The Nag Hammadi Library* EJ Brill, Leiden, 1977.

Szekely, Edmond and Weaver, Purcell (trans) *The Gospel of Peace of Jesus Christ by the disciple John* CW Daniel Company Limited, Ashingdon, England, 1937.

Smith, Robert *Edgar Cayce on Remembering your Past Lives* Aquarian Press, Wellingborough, 1990.

Sogyal Rinpoche *The Tibetan Book of Living and Dying* Rider, London, 1995.

Steiner, Rudolf *The Human Soul in Life and Death* The Rudolf Steiner Publishing Co, London, 1914.

– *Manifestations of Karma* Rudolf Steiner Press, London, 2000.

– *Karmic Relationships* Anthroposphical Publishing Company, London, 1957.

Encyclopaedia Britannica, 15th edition 1995, Encyclopaedia Britannica Inc, worldwide.

White, Ruth *Karma and Reincarnation* Piatkus, London, 2000.

Williston, Glen and Johnstone, Judith *Discovering Your Past Lives* Aquarian Press, Wellingborough, 1988.

Wood, Charlotte E *The Philosophy of Reincarnation* Theosophical Publishing House, London, 1927.

NOTES

Introduction

1   *Tibetan Book of Living and Dying* page 92.
2   Quoted in Soygal Rinpoche, page 92.
3   *Many Mansions* Gina Cerminara, Signet New American
      Library, 1978 edition, NY, page 60.

Chapter One

1   *A Study in Karma* Annie Besant, page 111.
2   Besant, page 112.
3   Dr Hiroshi Motoyama, *Karma and Reincarnation*, page 62.

Chapter Two

1   *The Hades Moon* Judy Hall, page 172 ff.

Chapter Three

1   *The Tibetan Book of Living and Dying*, page 95.
2   Cayce Reading 257, quoted in Smith, *Edgar Cayce on
      Remembering Your Past Lives*, page 29.
3   Quoted in Cerminara, *Many Mansions*, page 41.
4   Quoted in Steiner, *Manifestations of Karma*, page 19.
5   *New English Bible*, page 560.
6   Cerminara, page 127.
7   Steiner, *Manifestations of Karma*, page 185.
8   Ibid, page 193.
9   White, *Karma and Reincarnation*, page 91.
10   Newton, *Journey of Souls*, page 217.
11   Cerminara, page 91.
12   *Karma and Reincarnation* Dr Hiroshi Motoyama, pages 74–5.

Chapter Four

1   Steiner, *Manifestations of Karma*, page 169.

2   Plato, *Last Days of Socrates*, page 179.

3   Information sheet from the Bektashi museum, Nevshehir.

Chapter Five

1   Candlish, *The Revised Waite Compendium of Natal Astrology*, page 153.

2   Ibid, page 153.

3   Shantideva, *A Guide to the Bodhisatva's Way of Life*, trans. Stephen Batchelor (Dharamsala Library of Tibetan Works and Archives 1979), page 120.

4   Cerminara, *Many Mansions*, page 53.

5   Cerminara, page 47.

6   Cerminara, page 53.

7   Cerminara, page 87.

Chapter Six

1   Judy Hall, with additional material from Glen Williston and Judith Johnstone, in *Discovering your Past Lives*, The Aquarian Press, Wellingborough 1988, page 86.

2   Steiner, *Manifestations of Karma*, page 81.

3   Ibid, page 80.

4   See Judy Hall, *Patterns of the Past*.

5   Cerminara, *Many Mansions*, page 76.

6   Cerminara, page 11.

7   Steiner, page 67.

8   Steiner, page 66.

9   Cerminara, page 144.

10   Ibid, page 145.

Chapter Seven

1   Cerminara, *Many Mansions*, page 40.
2   Cerminara, page 185.
3   Cerminara, page 173.

Chapter Eight

1   Matthew 12:36.
2   Mark 7:22.
3   Luke 6:45.
4   Motoyama, *Karma and Reincarnation*, page 34.
5   Cerminara, *Many Mansions*, page 107.
6   Cerminara, page 107.

Chapter Nine

1   Reading 1436 quoted in Smith, *Edgar Cayce on Remembering your Past Lives*, page 43.
2   Judy Hall *Hands Across Time*, page 47 ff.
3   Cerminara, *Many Mansions*, page 123.
4   For a more detailed discussion see *Hands Across Time* and *Karmic Connections*.

Chapter Ten

1   Steiner, *Manifestations of Karma*, page 72.
2   Steiner, page 75.
3   Muller, ed, *Sacred Books of the East*, page 147 ff.
4   Jowett (trans), *Dialogues of Plato Volume I: Phaedo*, page 171.

5   Tredennick (trans), Plato's *Last Days of Socrates*, page 177.

6   *Pistis Sophia*, page 316 ff.

Chapter Eleven

1   Mascaro, *The Bhagavad Gita*, page 39.

2   Mascaro, page 79.

3   Muller, *Sacred Books of the East*, Volume 8, page 239.

4   Ibid, page 239.

5   Ibid, page 239.

6   Mascaro, page 75.

7   Mascaro, pages 74–5.

8   Interview on UK's Channel 4 *Kumbh Mela: the Greatest Show on Earth*, 14 January 2001.

9   Muller, *Sacred Books of the East*, Volume 45, page 170 ff.

10   Piyadassi, *Dependent Origination*, page 32.

11   *Buddhist Texts Through the Ages*, page 317.

12   *Encyclopaedia Britannica* 15, page 667.

13   The Majhima, verse 135, in Muller, M *Sacred Books of the East*.

14   Quoted in *Dependent Origination*, page 40.

15   Lodo, *Teachings: The Way of Death and Rebirth*, page 46.

16   *Sacred Books*, Volume 36, page 161 ff.

17   Ibid, page 164 ff.

18   Sogyal Rinpoche, *The Tibetan Book of Living and Dying*, page 198.

19   Ibid, page 215.

20   Forman and Quirke, *Hieroglyphs and the Afterlife in Egypt*, pages 110–1.

21   Christian Jacq, *The Black Pharaoh*, page 245.

22   Christian Jacq, *Magic and Mystery in Ancient Egypt*, page 101ff.

23   Jowett (trans), *Dialogues of Plato*, page 246 ff.

24   Jowett (trans), *Dialogues of Plato Volume I: Phaedo*, page 173.

25   Deuteronomy 28:58 ff, *New English Bible*.

26   Deuteronomy 30.

27   Leviticus 24:17–20.

28   Deuteronomy 14–15.

29   Translator Bryan Gundle.

30   *Yalkut Reubeni, No 1*, quoted in Head and Cranston, *Reincarnation: An East West Anthology*, page 26.

31   2 Esdras 2:27–30, *New English Bible*.

32   2 Esdras 2 ff.

33   2 Esdras 7:34–6.

34   2 Esdras 8:19–20.

35   Quoted in Head and Cranston, page 35.

36   Quoted in Head and Cranston, page 36.

37   Szekely (trans), *The Gospel of Peace of Jesus Christ by the disciple John*, page 34.

38   Szekely, page 37 ff.

39   Szekely, page 58.

40   *Pistis Sophia* Book 6:388, page 315 ff.

41   The Gospel of Thomas in *The Nag Hammadi Library*, page 123.

42   Romans 1:18–32.

43   Romans 2:5 ff.

44   Galations 6:7–10.

45   Luke 6:43–5.

46   Matthew 5:17 ff.

47   Matthew 5:27–8.

48   Matthew 7:12 ff.

49   Matthew 12:36.

50   Luke 6:20 ff.

51   John 9:12 ff.

52 Lattimore, *The New Testament,* page 218.

53 Blavatsky, *Secret Doctrine*, page 318.

54 Blavatsky, page 319.

55 Charlotte E. Woods, *The Philosophy of Reincarnation,* page 40.

56 Besant, *A Study in Karma*, page 1.

57 Ibid, page 4.

58 Ibid, page 5.

59 Ibid, page 32.

60 Ibid, page 89.

61 Ibid, page 69 ff.

62 White, *Karma and Reincarnation*, page 5.

63 *The Human Soul in Life and Death*, Rudolph Steiner Publishing Company, London (booklet, no date), page 13.

64 Steiner, *Manifestations of Karma*, page 2.

ABOUT THE
Author

An internationally-known author, lecturer and workshop leader, Judy Hall has been a karmic counsellor for over twenty-five years. During that time she has regressed over a thousand people to other lives. She is a well-respected and highly prolific author.

To contact Judy Hall for a karmic reading, please send an sae to her care of Thorsons.

Books by Judy Hall

Art of Psychic Protection (Findhorn Press and Samuel Weiser)
Deja Who? A Fresh Look at Past Lives (Findhorn Press)
The Hades Moon (Samuel Weiser)
Hands Across Time: the Soul Mate Enigma (Findhorn Press)
Holistic Menopause (Findhorn Press)
The Illustrated Guide to Astrology (Godsfield Press)
The Illustrated Guide to Crystals (Godsfield Press)
The Illustrated Guide to Divination (Godsfield Press)
Karmic Connections (The Wessex Astrologer)
The Karmic Journey: the birthchart, karma and reincarnation (Penguin Arkana)
Patterns of the Past: the birthchart, karma and reincarnation (The Wessex Astrologer)
Principles of Past Life Therapy (Thorsons)
Principles of Psychic Protection (Thorsons)
Principles of Reincarnation (Thorsons)
The Zodiac Pack: a visual approach to astrology (Findhorn Press)

Little Book of Karma

Richard Lawrence

The secret of success in every aspect of your life.

Karma is a fascinating subject that is crucial to everybody's lives. Richard Lawrence believes it is the key to complete success in mind, body and spirit. It is the basis of Eastern religion, but also runs through Western religions, especially Judaism.

little book of karma includes a brief introduction to Karma and its history, as well as short meditations on the nature of Karma. It also deals with instant Karma, action and reaction, sowing and reaping, minimising your problems, maximising your potential, give and take, lessons and service.

Richard Lawrence has written 3 books including the international bestseller Unlock Your Psychic Powers. He has been described as the UK's leading paranormal expert. He is also European Secretary of The Aetherius Society and a Director of the Inner Potential Centre in London.

Thorsons Way of Buddhism

John Snelling

Following on from First Directions, this new series provides a more in-depth, sophisticated introduction. An essential guide to the fastest growing spiritual practice in the West.

An increasing number of people in the West are seeking an authentic spirituality and becoming fascinated by Buddhism. Way of Buddhism provides a concise overview of the different forms of Buddhism, its practice and history, explaining who the Buddha was, the ideas and beliefs at the heart of Buddhism, how Buddhism has evolved and what it can offer us today. It also give guidance on how to meditate.

John Snelling, world renowned Buddhist scholar, died in 1991. He was general secretary of the Buddhist society, and editor of its journal The Middle Way, believed to be the most widely circulated Buddhist periodical in the world.

Thorsons *Way of Reincarnation*

Judy Hall

Following on from First Directions, this new series provides a more in-depth, sophisticated introduction. This is an accessible look at the different cultural and religious beliefs surrounding reincarnation.

Way of Reincarnation explains what reincarnation is and how and why people reincarnate, by looking at cultural and religious beliefs from around the world. It contains fascinating personal accounts and looks at the rise in belief today, giving examples of famous people throughout history who have believed in reincarnation, from Napolean and Mahler to Richard Gere and Princess Diana.

Judy Hall is an internationally known author, lecturer and workshop leader and has been a karmic counsellor for 25 years. Her books include Deja Who: A New Look at Old Lives and Hands Across Time (Findhorn Press), Principles of Past Life Therapy and The Karmic Journey: The Birthchart, Karma and Reincarnation (Penguin Arkana).

Thorsons Way of Psychic Protection

New Edition

Judy Hall

This is an exciting new introduction to the key techniques of psychic protection. It not only explores the history behind its use, and its intrinsic relationship with our natural environment, but includes practical, easy-to-use techniques.

Psychic protection explores the human need to open up consciousness and develop its unrealised potential against negative energies. This introductory guide combines practical, easy-to-use techniques, such as visualisations and flower essences, with actual case studies. It explains what psychic protection is and why it is necessary in the context of everyday life. It also looks at psychic attachment and how to guard against psychic attack.

Judy Hall is the author of twelve books including The Art of Psychic Protection (which has been translated into eleven languages including Romanian and Hebrew). She was trained in psychic protection by the late Christine Hartley (Dion Fortune's literary agent and Western-mystery tradition colleague). Judy has run psychic development groups for over twenty-five years. She is a workshop leader for The College of Psychic Studies in London and teaches psychic protection all over the world.

Karma, Reincarnation and Rebirth: How Karma affects our life, our personality, and our future

Diana St Ruth

An essential reader in understanding the cause and effect of Karma and how Karma can offer profound insight into our behaviour and personality.

Karma, Reincarnation and Rebirth goes beyond the concepts of birth and death. With compelling narrative, exercises and meditations, Diana St Ruth analyses this Buddhist natural law of Karma, offering us an understanding of how our Karma is key to our behaviour and the way we operate in the world. Essentially the law of Karma is the law of ourselves, the law of our inner lives. This book is a key to understanding ourselves on the deepest level.

It is structured as a series of short questions and issues around the topic, and each section is accompanied by an exercise to deepen the reader's understanding and personal development.

Diana St Ruth is a well known Buddhist teacher, and co-director of the Buddhist Publishing Group in Devon. She is the author of six books, including Little Book of Buddhist Wisdom (Element 1997) and Sitting (Penguin USA 1998).